CAMPING
IN KOREAN
NATIONAL
PARKS

Camping in Korean National Parks

Written by Beverlee Barnet
Photographs by Beverlee Barnet, Megan Andrew, and Korea National Park Service

Published by Seoul Selection
B1 Korean Publishers Association Bldg., 105-2 Sagan-dong,
Jongno-gu, Seoul 110-190, Korea
Tel: 82-2-734-9567
Fax: 82-2-734-9562
E-mail: publisher@seoulselection.com
Website: www.seoulselection.com

ISBN: 978-1-62412-000-8

Printed in the Republic of Korea

C**A**MPING
IN **KOREAN**
NATIONAL
PARKS

Beverlee Barnet

This book is dedicated to my loving father,
who taught me the joys of camping,
and to my beloved mother,
who has always demonstrated good sportsmanship.

Contents

p. 44

p. 72

p. 86

p. 178

Foreword

Since long ago, Korea's embroidery of beautiful mountains and rivers has earned it the description of a "silken tapestry of rivers and mountains." As beautiful as the whole is, its twenty national parks, representative examples of the country's beautiful natural environment, compare in their splendor to any other nation on Earth.

Recently, more and more people have opted for camping as a way of experiencing nature more closely and taking some time off from their everyday life. This has become especially common at the national parks, where the nature is particularly well preserved and the views are spectacular. Even foreign tourists are now coming to camp in ever-growing numbers.

Unfortunately, despite the increase in foreign tourists and residents in Korea, there has been little information available on camping at its national parks, and non-Koreans consequently know very little about it. It is vitally important that foreign readers with plans to visit Korea learn about its national parks and gain access to accurate information on camping.

This book goes into extensive detail on Korea's twenty national parks, offering introductions, maps, and information on campgrounds and other facilities. It also boasts over 250 photographs that allow readers a peak at the many charms of these parks, as well as details on other tourist sites near the national parks, delivering an even richer wealth of information on what visitors can do and see.

I want to thank Beverlee Barnet, who wrote this book based on her experiences visiting Korea's national parks over her 11 years in Korea. I hope that this book allows more foreign travelers to discover and enjoy the wonders of Korea's national parks.

Chung Kwang-soo
Chairman
Korea National Park Service

How to Use This Book

Information for Campers

Practical information is given on what campers can expect when camping in one of Korea's national parks and on how to prepare for a camping trip—from facilities and fees to transportation and emergency contacts.

Highlights

At a single glance, campers can read about the author's recommended points of interest in and around each national park. The highlights are accompanied by scenic photos which illustrate to the reader what to expect.

National Parks and Campgrounds

Descriptions are given on each park followed by an overview of campgrounds within that park. Campground profiles include on-site facilities and detailed directions on how to get there.

Map Symbols

Expressway	Mountain
Roadway	Temple / Templestay
49 Regional road number	Fortress
3 Route number	Mountain shelter
55 Expressway number	Beach
14 Interchange number	Harbor
Mountain national park	Ferry dock
Marine national park	Train / Subway station
Hiking trail	Park office / Ranger station
Campground	Visitor center

Campground Icons

- 🏠 Location
- 📞 Contact
- 🕐 Operational time
- 🏕️ Number of campsites
- 🚻 Pit toilet
- 🚹 Flush / chemical toilet
- ♿ Handicap toilet
- ♿ Wheelchair ramp to toilet
- 👶 Baby change table
- 🚿 Shower
- 🍳 Water/ field kitchen
- 💡 Electricity

- 🏕️ Tent platform
- 🍴 Food within walking distance
- 🪑 Picnic tables
- ℹ️ Visitor center or ranger station nearby
- 🚗 By car
- 🚕 By taxi
- 🚌 By bus
- 🚆 By train
- ✈️ By airplane
- ⛴️ By ferry

Korean Pronunciation

Many Korean words are long and difficult to pronounce when converted to English spelling. Where possible, hyphens are used in this book to divide the Korean word into managable segments as a way to help the reader with their Korean pronunciation and to make communication more effective. More specifically, the suffixes indicated below have been hyphenated:

Administrative Division Types

-do [도]   province or island
-si [시]   city area
-eup [읍]   town area
-gun [군]   county
-myeon [면] sub-county
-ri [리]   village area

Geographic Features

-san [산]   mountain
-bong [봉] peak
-bawi [바위] rock
-sa [사]   temple
-am [암]   hermitage
-po [포]   beach or port
-gang [강] river
-ho [호]   lake
-hang [항] port
-naru [나루] dock/wharf

11

Map of Korea

Introduction

The idea of lodging in a temporary shelter grew out of nomadic and pioneer lifestyles. Long ago, nomads and settlers used to pitch simple structures to protect themselves from threatening outdoor elements, but times and perceptions have changed. In present day, people turn to camping as a form of recreation. It is a way to escape from the concrete jungle, to be closer with nature, and to travel within financial means. Camping in Korean national parks answers all these needs, but it also offers a lot more.

Why Camp in Korean National Parks?

National parks are small to large regions that have been identified as unique land and sea settings worthy of preservation. Within Korea, there are twenty national parks. One is historical, showcasing valuable cultural properties from the Silla Dynasty (57 BC–935 AD); four are marine coastal parks protecting hundreds of kilometers of shoreline and marine life; and fifteen are mountain parks providing visitors with opportunities to become intimate with the country's natural landscape.

With the exception of historic Gyeongju National Park, all nineteen parks have campgrounds. National park campgrounds are situated near beautiful landscapes of blue sea, sandy beaches, waterfalls, towering forested mountains, or dramatic rocky pinnacles. And without exception, there are always Buddhist temples, inside or nearby the parks, with incredible artifacts and vibrant paintings. Most temples were constructed long ago and rest on forested mountainsides alongside crystal clear streams. National parks are like gems, showcasing Mother Nature while blending with the cultural spirit.

Since Korea is a mountainous country, hiking is a major pastime. There are well-marked hiking routes for all levels, from interpretive trails, village strolls, and temple exploration to rock scaling, ridge walks, and summiting. For those who like the beach, relaxation can be sought in other ways that might include a swimsuit and a good book.

In recent years, camping has become a favorite Korean vacation trend. As a result of this trend, national park campsites are well tended, offer clean and modern toilet facilities, have camping fees that are easy on the pocketbook, and are safe places. Since campgrounds are not isolated from village communities, visitors can enjoy both the rural and urban experience. This means that travelers have access to some great local cuisine.

Koreans have a close relationship with food and health. In the mountains, there is no shortage of village restaurants serving a smorgasbord of edible ferns, leaves, roots, and fungi, as in the dish *sanchae bibimbap* (*sanchae* literally means "mountain vegetables"). And in parks by the sea, soup bowls are often graced with octopus, squid, shrimp, and fish. Good, healthy food is available for the national park eating experience.

Not too long ago, it was difficult to get English-language information on national park campgrounds. In fact, most international visitors are unaware that Korea National Park Service operates recreational camping sites throughout the country. So this book was compiled for three reasons: first, to help international travelers find their way to national park campgrounds; second, to help visitors travel Korea in an affordable way; and third, to share with visitors the country's beautiful national park vistas. In the guidebook, there are easy-to-follow campground directions—by car, bus, and train. This guide makes national park camping more readily accessible to all.

Geography

South Korea (96,920 km²) is framed by three seas: the West Sea (also known as the Yellow Sea), the South Sea (East China Sea), and the East Sea (Sea of Japan). To the north is the Demilitarized Zone (DMZ), which separates the peninsula into South and North Korea. From the DMZ to Jeju Island, the total length of South Korea is 500 km, with a width of 220 km at its narrowest point. Off the coastline lie 3,400 islands, with Jeju Island as the largest (1,847 km²); Jeju is also home to the highest peak, Halla-san (1,950 m). This island is unique for its frost-free microclimate where citrus fruits grow, and for its ancient volcanic landmass. And although Korea is not an earthquake or volcano zone, hundreds of hot springs surface on Jeju and the mainland, many of which have been turned into health spas.

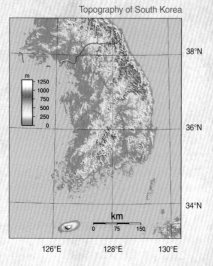

Topography of South Korea

The country is divided into nine provinces and seven self-governing cities. Its population recently hit 50 million. Almost half of the total populace lives in and around the capital city of Seoul. Within the peninsula, a complex network of superior roads and expressways criss-crosses the nation, linking large and small cities and making travel easy and efficient.

Climate

Korea has four distinct seasons. Korean winters are much shorter and less severe than those seen in countries like Russia and Canada. Temperatures fall below freezing from mid-December through mid-March and are cold enough for winter sports like downhill skiing and outdoor ice skating. Winter camping can get very cold, and those brave enough to do it must have all the proper gear.

Although it is mostly overcast, spring starts in March when trees start to bud. This season is plagued by microparticles of yellow dust carried on the air from China and Mongolia. Strong winds pick up desert dust and carry it across the West Sea to fall on the Korean Peninsula. For some spring days, it is recommended that you wear a mask over your nose and mouth. Otherwise, spring in Korea is very pleasant. The days are warm and the nights chilly, which makes for great camping and hiking.

Although a small amount of rain falls during the spring, the primary rainy season comes in the summer from mid-June to mid-August. Monsoons and passing typhoons in July mean that it can sometimes rain nonstop for days. If you want to go camping during this time, it is highly recommended that you bring a tarp to cover your tent for extra protection. You might also want to familiar yourself with the word *minbak* 민박. *Minbaks* are inexpensive rooms for rent that can be found around national parks and other tourist areas. Once the rain stops, the weather turns hot and humid. August is the most celebrated month among Koreans, when people flock to beaches, rivers, and campgrounds.

Another good time to camp is during the fall season from September to early November. Not only is the weather extremely fine, but the fall foliage in late October is beautiful, and the temperatures are the most comfortable for hiking. Koreans say that autumn is the time when "the sky is high and the horses are fat." This time of year, the nights are chilly and the days warm, with clear blue skies overhead

Climate Chart of Korea, 2008 (Korea Meteorological Administration)

	JAN	FEB	MAR	APR	MAY	JUN	JUL	AUG	SEP	OCT	NOV	DEC
Mean Temperature (°C)	-5	-2	4	11	17	22	25	26.5	21	14	7	-1
Precipitation (mm)	17	21	56	68	86	169	358	224	142	49	36	32
Relative Humidity (%)	64	64	64	63	66	73	81	78	73	63	68	66

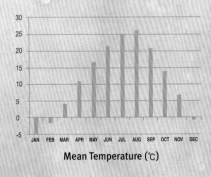

Mean Temperature (°C)

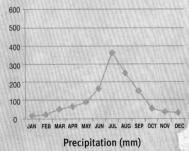

Precipitation (mm)

Information for Campers

Camping Environment

Three Types of Campgrounds

Campgrounds can be classified into three categories: auto, forested, and beach. With the more popular auto camping, users can park their car beside their tent in what looks like a large parking lot with trees. **Auto campgrounds** frequently offer wheelchair access and are family-oriented, with locations near restaurants and full services on offer. Most auto campgrounds are open all year round.

Forested campgrounds are small to large cleared areas in a natural forest setting located 15 m or more away from the parking facilities. They are slightly more isolated, and users must carry their camping gear onto the site. At forested campgrounds, services vary from basic to full. While some camps have only water and toilets, others have showers and electricity on top of the basic services. Operational times range from summer season only to all year round.

Beach campgrounds are small parcels of land by the sea. Some camps are located along the beachfront (sand or pebble) or in small forest areas behind the dunes. Natural terrain and campground design determine whether campers can park their car beside their tent. Services at beach campgrounds vary from basic to full. About half of these campgrounds operate for the summer season only, while the other half operate all year round.

Campsites

In many of the national park campgrounds, there are no specified numbered sites—when in this case, campers are expected to pitch their tents on designated cleared ground. As a result, during peak season, the campground takes on more of a chaotic appearance, with colorful tents in all shapes and sizes facing in all directions, erected one to two meters apart from one another. With the tents in such close proximity, don't be surprised if one of your neighbors invites you for conversation or even dinner. And although theft remains rare, it might be a good idea to place a small lock on your tent door if you are gone for an extended period of time.

When Koreans go camping, they don't do it in a small way. Typically, camping is a family event, which means lots of equipment. The campsite is a home away from home. The tent often covers at least three square meters, and the eating area is just as large, if not larger. Usually, one family takes up two campsites. That said, the tent capacities listed on the Korea National Park Service webpage tend to overestimate the total number of tents that can be accommodated at many of the campgrounds. The ones listed in this book do not coincide with those. Here, the number of tents per campground reflects the actual space occupied by users, available leveled ground for tent

pitching, and comfortable spacing.

Rarely will you find a grassy parcel of land, so it is highly recommended that you bring a ground sheet to place under your tent and a thermal foam mat (at least) to place under your sleeping bag. In some places, narrow valleys between mountains act like wind tunnels at certain times of the year, so it is highly recommended that you use a set of pegs to hold the tent in place. And in some national parks, raised square wooden platforms for tent pitching are installed in the campground for ground preservation purposes. On these platforms, rope is required to tie the tent down in case of a strong wind.

Facilities

Picnic Tables & Cooking

Since there are few picnic tables at the national parks, traditional Korean custom dictates sitting on the ground to feast. Large ground mats are commonly used for this. In the parks where there are picnic tables, they are usually positioned throughout the campground for

communal use, but more often than not are claimed by those who pitch their tent nearest to them. For safety reasons, parks prohibit the making of fire pits, but fuel burners and barbecues are used to create equally enticing meals.

Electricity

Electrical hookups (220 V) are usually found at auto campgrounds and service a handful of sites. The cost of using electricity is about 2,000 won per day; long extension cords are needed, since the electric boxes are centrally located and service multiple campsites. When there are no electric boxes, campers will sometimes use the bathroom outlet, but these outlets are not dependable, since hydro may or may not be turned on during the colder months of the year.

Water

Water is supplied at every campground, with taps located either at the outdoor kitchen or near the bathroom. Campground water is usually safe to drink, but not always. Any travelers who

question the water's purity would be advised to be safe and boil it. Mountain spring water can be found at many of the local temples, and you can also buy bottled water at a local store.

Showers

Showers at the parks are in the Korean style, which means one room with multiple shower heads. Unfortunately, there aren't too many shower facilities within the park system, and the ones that do exist operate only during the warmer months. There is one steadfast rule, however: the Korea National Park Service does not provide hot water (with the exception of the more popular auto campgrounds). Showers are cold and cost a small fee of 1,000 won.

Don't let this discourage you. There are other options available, like using public bathhouses or swimming pool showers to scrub down. Korea has a long and rich history connected to bathing. If you are looking for an authentic Korean experience, the bathhouse is not to be

missed. These facilities can be found everywhere, even in small towns. Korean bathhouses are separated by gender, and swimsuits are not permitted. Within the public bathhouse are pools ranging in temperature from very hot to ice cold, along with showers, steam rooms, saunas, and massage and body scrub services. Look for the words 사우나 (sauna) or 찜질방 (jjimjilbang). Some swimming pools have not only showers but also steam rooms and saunas. The Korean word for swimming pool is 수영장 (suyeongjang).

Toilets

Don't be surprised by the squat toilets! Over the past decade, Korea has been working hard to westernize its campground washrooms. Flush toilets in both pedestal and squat styles are available at most parks. Most of the bathroom blocks are newly constructed with white ceramic toilets and basins. In general, the bathrooms are clean and well maintained. New, more environmentally friendly chemical toilet trailers are

installed in places where there are no sewage lines. Pit toilets are used for winter camping when the water supply has been switched off, and they may also be used in selected campgrounds to minimize the human impact.

Wheelchair Accessibility

Korea has moved, and continues to move, into the forefront in recognizing and including the physically challenged, at least in campground toilet facilities. Well-graded ramps leading into large individual rooms with widened doors, lowered bars, a pedestal flush toilet, and a sink provide a welcome option. These facilities are big enough to accommodate the wheelchair and its passenger. Where individual rooms do not exist, you can find very large cubicles. In campgrounds that are open all year round, the bathroom blocks are locked up in the winter and replaced with portable pit toilets. This means that for wheelchair users, camping is limited to about six

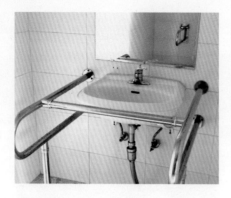

months of the year, from mid-April to late October.

Because Korea is mountainous, with a natural terrain of steep grades, stairs, and rocky surfaces, not all campground bathrooms cater to wheelchair users. However, the Korea National Park Service has designated at least one toilet block in selected auto campgrounds to accommodate wheelchairs. It is important to mention that these selected campgrounds are not perfect, with curbs and bumpy surfaces presenting challenges.

Garbage Disposal

Garbage disposal is a challenge even for Koreans. Trash and recycling bins are usually not provided, except at the more popular auto campgrounds. This means that campers must find a legitimate way to dispose their garbage. All too often, one sees a bag of trash left by the roadside.

Shelters

There are three national parks—Jiri-san, Seorak-san, and Deogyu-san—that have built shelters along extensive mountain hiking routes. For a small fee of 5,000 to 8,000 won per night per person, they provide a place to sleep, with some providing a blanket as well for an additional cost of about 1,000 won per night per person. Not all shelters sell food, so hikers will have to bring their own provisions. Weekends and peak season are busier than weekdays and low season. Shelter reservations can be made online (http://ecotour.knps.or.kr).

Operational Times

While all campgrounds are open during peak season (from July to August), there are some that are open between April to November, and others that are open all year round. Seasonal dates are posted under park signs. These dates indicate the seasons of spring (Apr. 1–May 31), peak summer (July 1–Aug. 31), and fall (Oct.

1–Nov. 30). An influx of campers can be expected in areas where cherry trees blossom, or where autumn colors are at their best.

Camping in Korea during peak season is a unique and eye-opening experience. Campgrounds are like tent cities, with tents pitched one to two meters apart from each other. If these conditions are not agreeable, travelers should consider camping during the off season from April to mid-June or from September to November. Camping off season has its benefits, with fewer tents, quieter campgrounds, cleaner bathroom blocks, and tent pads that are not so worn down.

Campsite Reservations

Usually, tent pitching is on a first come, first served basis. Note that auto campgrounds are more popular than forested campgrounds, where sites are more readily available. Auto camping is available on a reservation-only basis at the five most popular grounds: Hagam-po in Taean-haean National Park, Naewon and Deokdong in Jiri-san National Park, and Guryong and Geumdae in Chiak-san National Park. At the moment, the online camping reservation system on the Korea National Park Service website is in Korean only. Those who don't have an alien registration number or read Korean should book a campsite by telephone (02-3279-2700~1).

Fees

Fees can be divided into three categories: cultural heritage viewing fees, camping fees, and parking fees. Not all parks charge all three, and costs may vary slightly depending on the park and whether it's low or peak season. The prices quoted below are examples, and are subject to change at the Korea National Park Service's discretion.

National park admission is fundamentally free of charge, but you will have to pay a cultural heritage viewing fee when there are temples and other cultural relics within the park. These fees, when applicable, are paid at the ticket booth as you enter the gate.

Cultural Heritage Viewing Fees

(Unit: KRW)

Age	Fee
Adult (ages 19–64)	1,600–3,800
Youth (ages 13–18)	600–1,200
Child (ages 7–12)	300–600
Seniors (65+) Child (6 & under)	Free

Camping fees are generally charged per person per night, but for auto camping they are charged per vehicle per night (parking fees do not apply in this case). Typically, camping fees are collected at the ticket booth as visitors enter the campground.

Camping Fees
(Unit: KRW)

age	Off-Peak Season Fee	Peak Season Fee
Adult (ages 19–64)	1,600	2,000
Youth (ages 13–18)	1,200	1,500
Child (ages 7–12)	800	1,000

Auto Camping Fees
(Unit: KRW)

Car Type	Off-Peak Season Fee	Peak Season Fee
Passenger Car	9,000	11,000
Van (including camping van)	14,000	17,000

Parking fees are charged based on a nine-hour day and vehicle size. Visitors pay the fee at the ticket booth as they enter the public or camping parking lot.

Parking Fees
(Unit: KRW)

Car Type	Off-Peak Season Fee	Peak Season Fee
Compact car (below 1,000 cc)	2,000	2,000
Sedan or Van	4,000	5,000
Minibus (17 persons)	4,500	5,500
Tour Bus	6,000	7,500
Cargo vehicle (based on tonnage)	3,000–6,000	4,000–7,500

* Fee example for one adult during peak season (fees may vary depending on different factors.)

Cultural heritage viewing fee	3,800 won
Camping fee	2,000 won
Parking fee for a mid-size car	5,000 won
Total (per night)	10,800 won

* A separate but similar fee system applies in Halla-san National Park (see p.196).

Tent and Cabin Rentals

Small and large tents (5,000–8,000 won per day) and sleeping mattresses (2,000 won per day) are available for rent at specified parks during the peak camping season. All other camping equipment, including sleeping bags and cookware, must be supplied by the user.

Rental tents are usually pre-pitched in a designated area—more often than not, clumped together without access to scenic views. The tents are usually in good

condition, but there are no tarps to protect them from the rain, so they might leak during a heavy rainfall. A large thin sheet of plastic might be useful to pack. Forewarned is forearmed! To reserve a tent, call the park directly (see National Park Contact Information on p. 29).

Rental cabins are available at Deogyudae Campground in Deogyu-san National Park. This campground has small and large cottages for rent (peak season rates are 70,000–90,000 won per night). Reservations can be made online (http://ecotour.knps.or.kr).

Back Country Camping

Back country camping is strictly prohibited except in specified parks and in specified areas. Note that mountaineers will be charged a hefty fine for pitching their tent in an unauthorized area. Permits are required for rock climbers both to climb and to camp in their designated area of interest. Korea has some superb rock faces to scale.

Park Visitor Centers

Visitor centers are set up at many of the national parks, offering free history, wildlife, and agricultural exhibits. Some centers even have Internet access. At the information desk, staff members can answer questions regarding trails and provide maps. The downside is that almost all of the maps are in Korean.

Planning your vacation will require patience and thinking ahead. Your Korean hosts will be grateful if you make an effort to write down the places you want to visit within the national park. Communication is universal. If the park does not have a visitor center, information and maps can be acquired at a park ranger station located in the national park.

Templestay

Some Buddhist temples open their doors to foreigners who wish to experience Buddhist living in some very small way. Although programs vary from temple to temple, some participating temples offer a one-night, two-day training course. The agenda, strictly supervised by monks, might include an early morning rise for house cleaning, meditation, quiet mealtimes, a tea ceremony, and lotus flower making. Visitors interested in the Templestay program can refer to www. templestay.com. Note that not all temples

have the facilities for the program, nor do the participating temples offer the program regularly—reservations are mandatory. Jogye-sa, the biggest temple in Seoul, operates a comprehensive information center. Directions to Jogye-sa are available on the Templestay website.

Perceptions of Camping

Perceptions of camping in Korea are closely related to play. During peak season, the entire campground is lit from dawn to dusk, which makes for a long, long night when your neighbors prefer to play cards until the wee hours of the morning. One activity that is connected to camping is drinking of *makgeolli* (rice wine) and *soju*. On rare occasion, friendly Koreans swagger across the campground, and although Korea has a low crime rate, it is better to err on the side of caution.

National Park Management

Currently, nineteen out of twenty parks are managed by the Ministry of Environment under the direction of the Korea National Park Service (www.knps.or.kr). Halla-san National Park on Jeju Island is the only park overseen by a local government (www.hallasan.go.kr).

National parks adhere to five general restrictions:
- Parks are open from two hours before sunrise to two hours before sunset.
- Hiking is prohibited after sunset and during bad weather conditions.
- During the dry months (March–May), certain areas are restricted due to fire hazard.
- For visitor safety and natural preservation, hiking is permitted on marked trails only.
- Cooking, camping, and smoking are prohibited outside designated areas.

Camping Checklist

Packing the proper camping supplies can "make or break" your camping experience. A dry shelter, a safe place to set up camp, a warm bed, a dry change of clothes, good outerwear to protect you from the outside elements, and a good, hot meal do wonders for the human spirit.

Camping Equipment

- ☑ tent
- ☐ fly
- ☐ ground sheet
- ☐ tent pegs
- ☐ tent rope
- ☐ thermal mat
- ☐ sleeping bag (seasonal bag)
- ☐ flashlight
- ☐ eye mask (to block out night lamps)
- ☐ earplugs

Utensils

- ☐ lightweight water bottle
- ☐ gas burner with lighter
- ☐ cooking utensils (pots/cutlery)
- ☐ tablecloth
- ☐ detergent and scouring pad
- ☐ army knife
- ☐ camping towel

Protection

- ☐ first aid kit
- ☐ insect repellant/head net
- ☐ sunscreen
- ☐ sun hat
- ☐ sunglasses

Personal Effects

- ☐ hiking boots
- ☐ sandals
- ☐ shirts (long/short sleeves)
- ☐ shorts
- ☐ pants
- ☐ socks
- ☐ swimsuit (goggles/cap for pools)
- ☐ long underwear
  (sleepwear/top / bottom)
- ☐ waterproof jacket
- ☐ gloves/hat/scarf (spring/autumn)
- ☐ ski jacket/ski pants (spring/autumn)
- ☐ toiletry bag
  (toothbrush/paste/soaps, etc.)
- ☐ toilet paper

NATIONAL PARKS AT A GLANCE

Mountain Park

National Park	Campgrounds	Campsites	🚻	🚻	♿	🚣	🛒	🚿	🚰	⚓	🏊	🍴	⛱	❀	🏠	ℹ
Bukhan-san	1	30+	√										√	√		√
Chiak-san	3	149+	√	√	√	√		√	√	√		√	√	√		√
Deogyu-san	1	320+		√	√	√	√	√	√	√		√			√	√
Gaya-san	2	120+		√	√	√	√	√	√			√				√
Gyeryong-san	1	40	√					√	√			√		√		√
Halla-san	1	70	√	√	√		√	√		√	√	√		√		√
Jiri-san	9	575+	√	√	√	√	√	√	√	√	√	√	√	√	√	√
Juwang-san	1	50+	√	√		√	√	√	√			√				√
Naejang-san	2	90+	√	√	√	√	√	√	√			√	√	√		√
Odae-san	1	100+	√	√	√			√				√		√		√
Seorak-san	1	300+	√	√	√	√	√	√	√			√		√	√	√
Sobaek-san	2	120+	√	√	√	√		√	√	√	√	√	√	√		√
Songni-san	1	75+	√	√	√	√		√	√			√		√		√
Wolchul-san	2	45+	√			√	√				√	√		√		√
Worak-san	4	134+	√	√	√	√	√		√	√		√	√			√

Marine / Coastal Park

National Park	Campgrounds	Campsites	🚻	🚻	♿	🚣	🛒	🚿	🚰	⚓	🏊	🍴	⛱	❀	🏠	ℹ
Byeonsan-bando	2	130+	√	√	√	√	√	√				√	√	√		√
Dadohae-haesang	3	135+	√	√	√	√		√			√	√	√			√
Hallyeo-haesang	1	170	√	√	√	√	√	√	√			√				√
Taean-haean	1	70	√	√		√	√	√				√	√			√

Historical Park (Day use only)

National Park	Campgrounds	Campsites	🚻	🚻	♿	🚣	🛒	🚿	🚰	⚓	🏊	🍴	⛱	❀	🏠	ℹ
Gyeongju														√		

** ⛰ Total number of campgrounds   ⛺ Total number of campsites

National Park Contact Information
(english.knps.or.kr)

Mountain Parks

Bukhan-san	+82-02-909-0497~8 / +82-031-828-8000
Chiak-san	+82-033-732-5231
Deogyu-san	+82-063-322-3174~5
Gaya-san	+82-055-930-8000
Gyeryong-san	+82-042-825-3002
Halla-san	+82-064-713-9953 (Visitor center) / +82-064-756-9950 (Gwaneum-sa Office)
Jiri-san	+82-055-972-7771~2
	+82-063-625-8911~2 (Northern Office) / +82-061-780-7700 (Southern Office)
Juwang-san	+82-054-873-0018
Naejang-san	+82-063-538-7875~6
Odae-san	+82-033-332-6417
Seorak-san	+82-033-636-7700
Sobaek-san	+82-054-638-6196 / +82-043-423-0708 (Northern Office)
Songni-san	+82-043-542-5267~9
Wolchul-san	+82-061-473-5210~1
Worak-san	+82-043-653-3250

Marine / Coastal Parks

Byeonsan-bando	+82-063-582-7808
Dadohae-haesang	+82-061-554-5474
Hallyeo-haesang	+82-055-860-5800 / +82-055-640-2400
Taean-haean	+82-041-672-9737~8

Historical Park

Gyeonju	+82-054-741-7612~4

About the Korea National Park Service

The Korea National Park Service (KNPS) was founded in 1987. Today, it administers the country's national parks, including the mountains of Jiri-san and Seorak-san. It works to maintain a healthy natural ecosystem through preservation and restoration of natural resources, including endangered flora and fauna, as well as maintaining services to address any infrastructure that detracts from the environment. It develops and offers a range of visitor services, and is working to ensure safe and pleasant use of national park resources, by building and operating a comprehensive disaster safety management system. Affiliated with the Korean Ministry of Environment, it has a total of 26 regional offices in addition to its main headquarters and employs around 2,000 staff members, including research personnel.

TRANSPORTATION

Car

If you are traveling by car, one of the challenges is to overcome cultural differences in the concept of directions. Because Korea is a mountainous country, roads do not follow a straight grid pattern of north, south, east, and west. This can make orientation a challenge at times. However, all major roads and routes are numbered. Signs on highways and major roads are in both Korean and English. Most national park signs are in both languages, but travelers might encounter a slight variation in English spelling for the same Korean word—for example, the name of the mountain Jiri-san might also be spelled as "Chiri-san." The primary reason for spelling differences is a recent national switch from one phonetic system to another. Unfortunately, not all public and private signs were changed in the process.

Another point regarding road signs: sections of expressways are referred to by different names. For example, Expressway 35 is written as Jungbu Expressway in the north part of the country and Tongyeong-Daejeon Expressway in the south. The good news is that the expressway number doesn't change.

All expressways in Korea are toll roads. The toll is based on distance; travelers are issued a ticket upon entry and pay as they exit. By expressway, it takes about five hours to drive from the west to the east coast, and about five to six hours to drive from Seoul to the southern part of the peninsula.

Getting to national parks is relatively easy, although there are a number of possible routes. This book provides the most direct driving route from the nearest expressway. Alternative back roads—usually more scenic, but also more difficult to navigate—are left for the traveler to strategize.

Car Rental: To rent a car, travelers must have a passport, be at least 21 years old, and hold an international driver's license or a Korean driver's license. International licenses can only be obtained in your home country. Insurance is mandatory for all drivers. It is also recommended that you purchase full liability insurance, as Korea has a high accident rate. The driving system is the same as in North America and Europe, with the steering column on the left side.

The following is a list of websites where travelers can book a car online.

Avis	www.avis.com
Hertz	www.hertz.com
National Car	www.nationalcar.com
Budget	www.budget.com
Kumho	www.kumhorent.com

Bus

In Korea, express and intercity bus companies operate an extensive network throughout the entire country. Transportation is comfortable, safe, frequent, affordable, and punctual. Bus terminals in major cities like Seoul, Daejeon, Daegu, Gwangju, and Busan have direct routes to some national parks; more often, however, they connect with a nearby city transfer point, where travelers can board a more frequently run local bus. In smaller cities, express and intercity bus terminals often share the same building. This makes for an easy transfer—often easier and faster than train travel.

Nambu, Central City, Gangnam Express, and East (Dong) Seoul are the four major bus terminals in Seoul. Bus Terminal Complex, Dongbu Gyeongnam Intercity, and Seobu Intercity are the three major bus terminals in Busan. Intercity and express bus services operate from these terminals. Advance ticket purchase is available but often unnecessary due to the frequent bus departures.

Taxi

Taxi services in Korea are affordable and provide an efficient way of getting from point A to point B. In rural areas, taxi stands are usually located near bus terminals and train stations. Rural taxi drivers are familiar with driving routes into national parks, as they often transport campers and hikers to campgrounds and trailheads. When driving within city limits, they use the meter, but if a passenger wants to go to a place where a driver won't get a return fare, a flat rate is charged. It is not difficult to find a taxi, nor are they difficult to flag down. However, communication might be a challenge. Passengers should write down their destination in Korean to eliminate confusion (refer to the Essential Korean for Campers on p. 199 and Interpretation Services on p.35).

Train

Korea Railroad (better known as KORAIL) operates several lines: Gyeongbu, Honam, Jeolla, Janghang, Jungang, Donghaenambu, Gyeongjeon, Chungbuk, and Taebaek. Ticket prices differ for class (first and economy) and the choice of train.

The affordable high-speed rail system KTX (Korea Train Express) operates between Seoul and Busan and between Seoul and Mokpo. With speeds up to 300

km/h, the travel time from Seoul to Busan is now two hours and fifty minutes. Constant upgrades are under way, and new KTX lines are being opened. For further information on KORAIL routes, refer to www.korail.com.

This book provides information about the nearest train station to the campground, under the heading of the national park and the campground name. In small towns, train stations are often close to bus terminals. Travelers will need to get themselves from the train station to the local bus terminal where buses go to and from the national park.

Korea Rail Pass: Travelers can purchase a KR Pass anywhere around the world from overseas travel agents or online. The pass offers unlimited regular and KTX rail travel for three, five, seven, or ten consecutive days at a cost of 84,600 won, 127,000 won, 160,400 won, or 185,100 won, respectively. Children under the age of four travel free. Children aged four to twelve get a 50% discount. Young people from the ages of 13 to 25 are also entitled to a discount with the

required identification. There is also a "Happy Rail Pass" available to foreigners living in Korea, which can be purchased on the KORAIL site.

Airline

The following airlines service cities within Korea. Travelers can book flights online through the website.

Korean Air	www.koreanair.co.kr
Asiana Airlines	www.flyasiana.com
Jeju Air	www.jejuair.net
Eastar Jet	www.eastarjet.com
Jin Air	www.jinair.com
T'way	www.twayair.com
Air Busan	www.flyairbusan.com

Ferry

Ferries depart from Mokpo Coastal Ferry Terminal 목포연안여객터미널 and Paengmokhang 팽목항 and service the outer southwestern islands (Dadohae-haesang National Park) and Jeju Island. Note that there are 1,700 islands and islets in this region. For obvious reasons, not all ferry companies or islands are listed. Local ferries stop at several islands en route, dropping off passengers before making a return trip. You can also visit http://island.haewoon.co.kr to see a schedule for all ferries operating in Korea and to book tickets. Unfortunately, this service is not available in English at this time.

The following is a list of ferry companies with their contact numbers.

Mokpo Coastal Ferry Terminal

Hong-do, Heuksan-do
Namhae Express Co. Ltd.
061-244-9915~6
Dongyang Express Co. Ltd.
061-243-2111~4

Jeju-do
Sea World Co. Ltd (www.seaferry.co.kr)
061- 243-1927~8

Bigeum-do, Docho-do, Anjwa-do, Palgeum-do, Amtae-do, Jaeun-do
Daeheung Corporation
061-244-0005

Jangsan, Sangtae, Haui-do, Jo-do
Joyang Transportation Co. Ltd.
061-244-0038, 6038

Jangsan-do, Sangtae-do, Haui-do
Jindo Transportation Co. Ltd.
061-242-4520, 9542

Goha-do, Dal-do, Oedal-do, Nul-do (Yul-do)
Shinjin Shipping 061-244-0522

Paengmok-hang

Gwanmae-do
Jodo Nonghyup Ferry 061-542-5383
HL Haewoon Ferry 061-544-0833

HEALTH AND SAFETY

Medical Information

Vaccinations are not required before entering the country, as Korea is free of serious diseases. This is not to say, however, that travelers should not buy travel insurance as a precaution. Accidents do happen. It is also a good idea to consult your government travel health website or the World Health Organization (www.who.int) for updates on recent medical alerts.

The quality of medical care in Korea depends on your location. In metropolitan regions, medical care is up to Western standards. At large city hospitals, physicians communicate in English, but treatment in rural areas can be lacking in quality, and language may present a barrier.

Since pharmaceuticals in Korea differ from those in the West, travelers requiring medication should bring a full supply during their stay. Medications should be in their original packaging and clearly labeled. It's also a good idea to bring letters from doctors documenting medical necessity or stating a medical condition. Over-the-counter medications such as Tylenol, throat lozenges, bandages, and antibiotics for diarrhea can be purchased at local pharmacies. Pharmacies are marked with the word 약 (*yak*) and can be found everywhere, even in bus terminals.

The following are contact numbers for medical services in Seoul. Unfortunately, international clinics are not located near national parks, but park rangers should be able to assist with medical emergencies. National Emergency Medical Services can be reached by dialing 119.

Severance Hospital, International Clinic
(in Sinchon, Seoul)
02-361-6540
http://sev.iseverance.com

Samsung Medical Center & International Health Service (in Gangnam, Seoul)
02-3410-0200
www.samsunghospital.com

Seoul International University International Healthcare Service
(in Hyehwa, Seoul)
02-2072-2890
www.snuh.org

International Clinic in Itaewon, Seoul
02-790-0857
www.internationalclinic.co.kr

Mobile Phone Rental

At Incheon and Gimpo International Airports, mobile phones are available for rent at a low daily rate. It is worth considering carrying a phone while traveling, just in case there are any unexpected events.

Dangers

Is camping safe in Korea? At one time in recent history, tigers and bears used to roam the mountains. But after Japanese colonization from 1910 to 1945, deforestation, and the Korean War from 1950 to 1953, there is now little large wildlife left. Wild boars, small mountain goats, and deer are about all there are after half a century of turmoil.

Jiri-san National Park is going to great lengths to reintroduce the Asiatic black bear. No other national park in the country is large enough to accommodate both animal and man. The park now has 27 bears, with the newest cubs born in 2012. This park offers extensive back country hiking trails, and precautions should be taken lest your path cross with that of a bear or wild boar.

With other wildlife, it is recommended that you use your discretion. Bring your shoes into your tent at night just in case a snake or spider is looking for a warm place to settle. Snakes in Korea are small (like the meter-long venomous short-tailed viper), but their strike can still be deadly. If provoked, a snake will bite. These creatures require space to make their escape. It is best just to leave them alone. Spiders prefer to build webs above ground, but they can still bite.

Mosquitoes are pesky everywhere around the world, so it might be a good idea to bring a skin repellant. Areas marked with malaria warnings are usually around the border between South and North Korea. Other annoyances might include the wildcats and stray dogs that occasionally wander around campgrounds looking for food scraps.

QUICK REFERENCE

Tourist Information Services

KTO Tourist Information Center (www.visitkorea.or.kr)

The Tourist Information Center in Seoul, operated by the Korea Tourism Organization (KTO), carries free national park brochures and maps in English. The center has friendly and helpful staff members who can help travelers make reservations for ferries or book a campsite at one of the more popular national parks. To get to KTO, take Seoul Subway Line 1 to Jonggak Station and head out of Exit 5.

1330 Call Center

Another helpful service is KTO's Information Call Center. For general inquiries, dial the provincial area code followed by 1330. Operators offer language services in English, Japanese, Chinese, and Korean. In Seoul, this service operates 24 hours a day.

Area Code	Province
02	Seoul
031	Gyeonggi
032	Incheon
033	Gangwon
041	Chungcheongnam
042	Daejeon
043	Chungcheongbuk
051	Busan
052	Ulsan
053	Daegu
054	Gyeongsangbuk
055	Gyeongsangnam
061	Jeollanam
062	Gwangju
063	Jeollabuk
064	Jeju

Interpretation Services

If interpretation is what you need, then telephone Before Babel Brigade (BBB), a free interpretation service operated by volunteers to help foreigners with communication. BBB volunteers are available for sixteen languages. Dial 1588-5644 for interpretation services.

Internet

Korea is one of the most Internet-friendly countries in the world. Free web access is available at post offices, tourist information centers, libraries, and national park visitor centers. PC rooms, which let you use a computer for a small fee of up to 2,000 won per hour, can be found in small and large towns and cities. These rooms are often located on the second floor or higher. Look for the sign reading PC 방 (*PC-bang*).

NORTHWEST

GYEONGGI-DO | CHUNGCHEONGBUK-DO | CHUNGCHEONGNAM-DO

Bukhan-san National Park

Sobaek-san National Park

Worak-san National Park

Taean-haean National Park

Songni-san National Park

Gyeryong-san National Park

Bukhan-san
National Park

북한산 국립공원

Highlights

1. Enjoy breathtaking views of **white granite peaks.**

2. Follow the forested foothill paths of **Dulle-gil Trail** 둘레길.

3. Hike along the wall of **Bukhan-san Fortress** 북한산성 or visit one of the **temples.**

4. Sign up with an alpine rock climbing group and camp at the base of beautiful **Insu-bong** 인수봉, which is the only national park campground in Korea designated as only for rock climbers.

Don't be put off by the five million visitors who come to hike Bukhan-san yearly. Usually in the afternoon, floods of people scout out the park's multiple trails. No exaggeration here—hikers might come across a traffic jam or two while climbing or squeezing between rocks on a hiking course. Bukhan-san is popular for two primary reasons. One, it is the closest national park to Seoul, offering Seoulites a quick escape from their daily lives in the congested city on weekends. The second reason is simply the majestic beauty of the bald, white granite mountain peaks. Although there are many trails to enjoy, the most popular routes include Baegundae 백운대 (Bukhan-san's highest peak at 837 m), the fortress wall, and the breathtaking Insu-bong 인수봉, which rises to 810.5 m. Along the Insu-bong trail, you can stop at the base of the mountain and look up at climbers on ropes scaling the rock face. This sport is best described as sheer excitement.

One of the many great features of this park is a trail designed for those who don't want a difficult trek. The 70-kilometer Dulle-gil Trail 둘레길 is made up of

a series of connecting forested paths along foothills and villages, numbering 21 sections in total. This leisurely nature hike roughly follows the park's perimeter, and trail sections are easily accessible by public transit.

Another great feature of the park is Bukhan-san Fortress 북한산성, which was built in 1711 as a place of retreat for imperial rulers forced to abandon their city residence in emergency situations. This fortification, which boasts 120 rooms, stands independent of the capital city. The fortress has fifteen gates attached to its walls (eight kilometers long and seven meters high), which follow the contours of the mountain ridges, making it difficult for enemies to get in. Visitors can hike alongside the sections of the fortification.

Another highlight of the park is Hwagye-sa 화계사. Zen Master Seung Sahn, an active proponent of Buddhism in the West, opened the Hwagye-sa International Zen Center in 1994. This temple is home to a respected community of Western monks. For foreigners, there are dharma talks and meditation sessions on Sundays. Long retreats and an English-language Templestay program are available at this location.

Hwagye-sa 화계사 (02-902-2663, www.hwagyesa.org)
Jingwan-sa 진관사 (02-388-7999, www.jinkwansa.org)

Hwagye-sa

Insu
Campground
인수 야영장

⌂ San 1-1 Jeongneung 4-dong,
  Seongbuk-gu, Seoul
☎ 02-996-5306
⏱ Open all year round

⊲ 30+	⚇	✓	⚥	♿	♨	⛼	🚿
⛲	⚡	⊴	🍴	⛺ ✓	ⓘ ✓		

There is just one campground in Bukhan-san National Park lying at the base of Insu-bong. The campground can accommodate 30 tents comfortably, though the park claims it can accommodate up to 70. During peak season, it gives a whole new meaning to the phrase "love thy neighbor." Small gravel platforms have been constructed among large boulders in the campground to house small tents.

TIP

How to Get a Camping and Climbing Permit

This campground is designated as only for rock climbers. To get a camping and climbing permit, contact the Korean Alpine Federation at 02-414-2750 (www.kaf.or.kr) or the Korean Alpine Club at 031-855-8848 (www.cac.or.kr).

Insu-bong, Bukhan-san National Park

In the upper section of the campground, a public hiking trail passes between tent sites. If privacy is important, campers should consider setting up camp below the rescue center. Located at the parking lot are shops, restaurants, and a ranger station where trail maps are available. Unless campers want to make daily hikes (40 minutes one way) to and from restaurants, they should pack their own provisions. Near the campground is a mountain stream, but water purity is questionable.

Transport Info From Seoul Ring Expressway 100, take Exit 14 (Uijeongbu Interchange) and follow the right ramp toward Seoul (not Uijeongbu). Go straight along Dong 1 lo 동1로 (also spelled as Tong-il-ro) through multiple intersections. Turn right onto Banghangno 방학로 (Banghak-no) and drive over the Sanggyegyo Bridge 상계교. Follow this route for multiple intersections into the mountain region. At the end of this road, there will be two landmarks, a police station and a U-turn. Follow the U-turn and take the first right turn (less than 100 m from the police station) onto an unlikely looking mountain road. The bus terminal is situated at the bottom of this road. Along this road are two parking lots. One is halfway up, and the other is near the top just below the temple of Doseon-sa 도선사. The campground is a 40-minute hike from the upper parking lot.

 The terminal at the bottom of the mountain road services two bus routes.
a) Bus No. 109 stars from Gwanghwamun and stops near Hyehwa Subway Station (Line 4).
b) Bus No. 120 starts from Cheongnyangni (Line 1), and stops near Wolgok (Line 6), Mia (Line 4), and Suyu (Line 4) subway stations en route.

 Take the subway to Banghak Station (Line 1). It is a short ride by taxi to the upper parking lot just below Doseon-sa.

Sobaek-san
National Park

소백산 국립공원

Highlights

1. Hike to the peak of **Biro-bong** 비로봉, where a gorgeous meadow summit awaits.

2. Climb through Danyang district's **Gosu Cave**고수동굴, with its stalagmites, ladders, and creative mood lighting. A fun activity for all, but especially for children.

3. Enjoy some fun-for-the-whole-family rafting along the **Namhan-gang** 남한강 near the village of **Osa-ri** 오사리.

4. Visit the beautiful temple of **Guin-sa** 구인사, which is set in a forested mountain crevasse.

5. Tour the temple of **Buseok-sa** 부석사, where a thousand-year-old structure still stands to this day.

6. Across from Gosu Cave, a roadside stand has been in business for years selling the **best honey** around.

The trail to Biro-bong, Sobaek-san National Park

Sobaek-san National Park, which straddles the border of Chungcheongbuk-do and Gyeongsangbuk-do, is part of the Sobaek Mountain Range 소백산맥. The name means "small white mountain," but visitors should not underestimate its size. On the contrary, there are several peaks that reach up to over 1,200 m, with the Baekdu Daegan 백두대간—the 735 km trail along Korea's mountainous spine—running through the entire length of the national park. Most hikers, however, only go to and from the highest peak, Biro-bong 비로봉 (with a summit at 1,439 m). This breathtaking meadow hilltop is covered with azalea flowers in the spring, and people come from far and wide during this season to photograph its poetry.

But not all visitors come to Sobaek-san to hike. The district of Danyang 단양 hosts a wide array of activities, ranging from river rafting, paragliding, and fly fishing to clay shooting, water park enjoyment, cave exploring, and touring of the Eight Scenic Wonders of Danyang 단양8경 (see p. 54). Most places can be reached on foot, by bus, or by car.

Within the park locality are three notable Buddhist temples: Huibang-sa

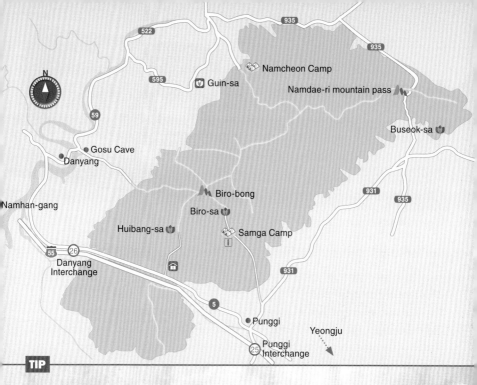

TIP

Suggested Route

Route 5 (Huibang-sa) → Regional Road 931 (Samga Campground, Biro-bong, Buseok-sa) → Regional Road 935 (mountain pass to Namdae-ri) → Regional Road 522→ Regional Road 595 (Namcheon Campground, river rafting, Guin-sa) → Route 59 (Danyang, Gosu Cave, Biro-bong)

희방사, Buseok-sa 부석사, and Guin-sa 구인사. The last of these is a revival by the Cheontae Order of Korean Buddhism that was reestablished in 1945. The architecture of the buildings is stunning, and the temple location is scenic. In contrast to Guin-sa, Buseok-sa has some of the oldest surviving relics around and is highly regarded as one of the country's top-ranked historic temples.

This national park is home to two campgrounds: Namcheon 남천, located in the northeast corner of the park, and Samga 삼가, located in the southwest corner. With a good road atlas, it is possible to drive the perimeter of the park while taking in local sights. Take note: the mountain pass to Namdae-ri 남대리 is a narrow single-lane road that was not built for camping vans, trailers, or inexperienced drivers.

🅥 Guin-sa (043-420-7323, http://temple.cheontae.org)

Namcheon
Campground
남천 야영장

⌂ San 60-1 Namcheon-ri,
   Yeongchun-myeon, Danyang-gun,
   Chungcheongbuk-do
📞 043-421-0721, 043-423-0708
🕐 July to August

This forested campground is located at the end of Namcheon Valley 남천계곡.
Divided into two primary sections (separated by a 50-meter boardwalk),
Namcheon has six tent platforms, two outdoor kitchens, and a few picnic tables
scattered around the campground. The dirt-surface tent pads are roped off,
with one site just next to the other. The bonus to this location is its proximity to
Guin-sa—it makes for a lovely day walk. Campers should pack their own food
and bring a head net for protection. In the humid months of July and August,
this area attracts pesky flies.

Transport Info From Jungang Expressway 55, take Exit 26 (Danyang Interchange) and follow
Route 5 going north to Danyang. Turn onto Route 59 through Danyang and over the
arched bridge. Route 59 turns left just after the bridge and snakes its way through
the mountains and along the river. Continue to follow this route onto Regional Road
522, and then Regional Road 595. Follow the signs to Namcheon Campground,
which is at the end of Namcheon Valley. (Note: Regional Road 595 is a loop road
and has two access points. Bypass the first access point unless you wish to take a
longer, more scenic mountain drive.)

🚌 a) The bus stop for Namcheon Campground is located 300 m from Danyang
Express Bus Terminal. Walk to the arched bridge road, turn left, and walk halfway
up the hill. The bus stop is in front of an apartment building. These buses are not
numbered, so it is best to write down the name of your destination and ask the bus
driver before boarding. Campers should take the Yeongchun 영춘 bus (eight times
daily) for Namcheon Campground. Once in Yeongchun, campers will have to walk
3 km along a country road or hail a cab to get to the campground.

b) Buses depart East Seoul Bus Terminal for Guin-sa twelve times daily. Namcheon
Campground is only a ten-minute taxi ride from Guin-sa.

🚆 The nearest train station is Danyang Station which is located 5 km from Danyang
Express Bus Terminal.

Located just minutes from the town of Punggi 풍기, this small campground is a popular family destination for a number of reasons. Besides having easy town access, it is at the trailhead of Biro-bong and a short distance from the temple of Biro-sa 비로사. The toilet facilities are new, large, and clean, built with the specific intent to service families and the physically challenged. Tents are erected on sandy gravel, with a manmade stream separating the more popular back section from the front. Electric units are installed throughout the campground. This campground is a 500-meter walk from the park's bus stop.

Samga
Campground
삼가 야영장

🏠 302-1 Samga-ri, Punggi-eup, Yeongju-si, Gyeongsangbuk-do
📞 054-637-3794
🕐 Open all year round

Transport Info 🚗 From Jungang Expressway 55, take Exit 25 (Punggi Interchange). Turn right at the T-intersection and follow the road sign for about one kilometer going toward Punggi. Turn right again at the sign for Buseok 부석. Go straight for 2 km. Drive under the concrete railway bridge and turn left. Follow the brown and white signs to Biro-sa. The campground is located just before Biro-sa along a small country road northeast of Punggi.

🚌 Bus No. 26 departs from Yeongju 영주 and Punggi eight times daily. This bus route is circular; it starts in Yeongju and goes through Punggi, stopping at the train station on its way to Samga-ri. Other buses depart from Seoul (six times daily), Suwon (twelve times daily), and Incheon (twelve times daily) for the Punggi bus stop, which is located 50 m from the train station.

🚆 The nearest train station is Punggi Station, which is located downtown (50 m from the Punggi bus stop).

🚕 Taxis charge a rate of about 12,000 won to go from Punggi Station to the campground. It's about a ten-minute ride.

Worak-san
National Park
월악산 국립공원

Highlights

1. Visit the beautiful **Mireuksaji** 미륵사지 **temple site** during the Buddha's Birthday holiday, when the hundreds of multicolored lanterns hanging from above are illuminated at night.

2. Climb the colorful restored **Deokju-san Fortress** 덕주산성 gate, or go up to **Deokju-sa** 덕주사, where the Buddha's image has been carved into a large rock face.

3. Hike any of the **majestic, craggy peaked mountains**. Many of the hiking routes have ropes, ladders, and rungs, providing an exhilarating hiking experience.

4. Ride the ferry at **Janghoe-naru** 장회나루 on **Chungju-ho** 충주호. This round-trip ride takes visitors through the mountainous region.

5. Taste the local mountain vegetable cuisine at one of the park village restaurants. One favorite dish is *sanchae bibimbap* 산채비빔밥.

6. Spend a day in **Suanbo village** 수안보 and soak in the natural mineral hot springs. This village hosts a spring blossom festival during the latter half of April.

The defining features of this park are its craggy peaks and sparklingly clear valley rivers. Hikers from across the country climb its mountainous trails every weekend. Hordes of buses from Seoul and other places fill the parking lots in the early morning, leaving in the late afternoon with their weary passengers. The three main hiking courses at Worak-san National Park are Yeong-bong 영봉 (1,097 m), Mansu-bong 만수봉 (985 m), and Dorak-san 도락산 (962 m). These craggy mountains provide a suitable habitat for the twenty rare mountain Amur Goral goats that are part of the new breeding program within the park.

If you are not a hiker but still wish to cultivate the spirit within, seek out Mireuksaji 미륵사지 temple site and Deokju-sa 덕주사, the park's two representative Buddhist cultural properties, or wade in the shallow waters of the cool, crystal clear mountain rivers. In the spring, the national park is a veritable painter's palette with splashes of pink on mountainsides and blossom-lined roads. The park's fall foliage is just as beautiful.

Lake Chungju-ho 충주호 and its main tributary Namhan-gang 남한강 are surrounded by elevated peaks and impressive cliffs best viewed from one of the ferries at Janghoe-naru

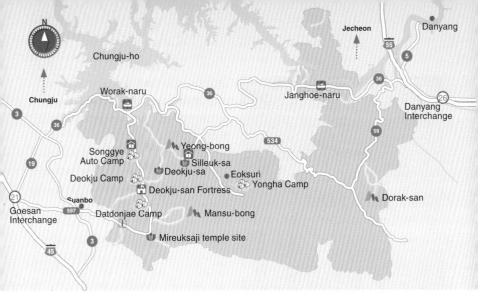

장회나루, which is situated 9 km west of Route 59. Two of the Eight Scenic Wonders of Danyang 단양8경—Oksun-bong 옥순봉 and Gudam-bong 구담봉—can be viewed from the cruise (see p. 54). Another tourist sight further along the river on the Janghoe ferry route is the Cheongpung Cultural Heritage Complex 청풍문화재단지. This open museum is a collection of household artifacts and heritage buildings taken from the region before it was flooded in 1985. Below the museum, tourists can also walk on a stage set of an authentic-looking Korean village of yesteryear. It is possible for passengers to disembark from their boat, tour the museum, and catch the next boat back to the wharf. To avoid getting stranded, travelers

Amur Goral, Worak-san National Park (top)
Winter scenery of Gudam-bong, seen from Janghoe-naru (bottom)

should check the return schedule before disembarking. Another, less scenic ferry also tours Chungju-ho. Its wharf is at Worak-naru 월악나루, about 5 km north of Songgye Auto Campground where Regional Road 597 and Route 36 meet. Of the two ferry services, Janghoe-naru has more to offer.

Worak-san operates four campgrounds in total. None of the park's

Maitreya Buddha image carved into a rock face at Deokju-sa

campgrounds has showers, but you can scrub down at any of the hot spring bathhouses and spas in the popular village of Suanbo 수안보, which is located just 12 km from the hub of Songgye Valley 송계계곡. In winter, Suanbo also operates a ski run; the hot springs are a great way to warm up after a day of skiing. Public buses run between Songgye Valley and Suanbo.

Worak-san is a large park located between Expressways 45 and 55. It takes about one hour to drive from one side of the park to the other along winding Route 36. This road runs east-west to the north of the park boundary, linking the two expressways. All campgrounds are accessible from this route. For those who want to hike Dorak-san, buses depart nine times daily from Danyang (the bus stop is beside the arch bridge). There are two private campgrounds along Route 59 just north of Dorak-san.

> **TIP**
>
> **Eight Scenic Wonders of Danyang** 단양8경
> These scenic sights include interesting natural land formations with stories attached, as well as rock formations that resemble figures, like a swimmer or a rainbow. Six are located within Worak-san, and two are northwest of the town of Danyang 단양. One story (that of Dodamsam-bong 도담삼봉) tells of a love triangle among a husband, wife, and concubine. The island peak formation is said to show the wife looking away from her husband because he took a concubine to bear a son, something his wife was unable to do.

Datdonjae
Campground
닷돈재 야영장

⌂ 70-2 Mireuk-ri, Suanbo-myeon,
   Chungju-si, Chungcheongbuk-do
📞 043-653-3250
🕐 Open all year round

This campground is situated in a pretty forested area 20 to 50 m back from Regional Road 597. The forest is primarily pine, with some of the prettier campsites set along the river. There are three clean washrooms, three outdoor kitchens, and one very large parking lot. Part of this campground (by the parking lot) is wheelchair-accessible.

🔊 25+	🚻 ✓	🧍 ✓	♿ ✓	🛋 ✓	🚌 ✓	⚓
🚰 ✓	♨	〰	🍴 ✓	⛩	ℹ

Transport Info From Jungbu Inland Expressway 45
a) Take exit 21 (Geosan Interchange) and follow Regional Road 597 through Suanbo to Worak-san.
b) Take exit 21 (Geosan Interchange) and follow Route 19 onto Route 3 going south for 1 km toward Suanbo. Turn left onto and follow Route 36 for about 15 km. Make a right turn onto Regional Road 597.

From Jungang Expressway 55
c) Take exit 26 (Danyang Interchange) and follow Route 5 going north. Turn left onto and follow route 36 to the other side of the park. Turn left onto Regional Road 597.

 Buses depart from Chungju Bus Terminal (bus No. 246 goes through Suanbo to Datdonjae and Deokju Campgrounds—catch the bus outside of the terminal by the taxi stand—five times daily). Other buses depart from East Seoul (nine times daily) and Jecheon (six times daily) for Songgye Valley.

 The nearest train stations are Chungju Station (located 1 km from Chungju Bus Terminal) and Jecheon 제천 Station. To get to the Jecheon bus stop go six traffic lights uphill from the train station. The bus stop is next to a U-shaped glass-front building.

Deokju
Campground
덕주 야영장

⌂ 131 Songgye-ri, Hansu-myeon, Jesheon-si,
  Chungcheongbuk-do
☎ 043-653-3250
⏲ Open all year round

Deokju Campground is located across from Deokju village. In the village there are several restaurants, *minbaks*, a trailhead leading to Deokju-sa, a bus stop, and a large parking lot for tour buses and cars. At this campground some sites are sandwiched between the road and river, while other more private sites sit further back on the hillside. There are two new large bathroom blocks at the back of the property. These washrooms are locked during winter. For those wanting to camp during the colder months, the public facility in the parking lot across the street remains open.

Transport Info See Datdonjae Campground.

This campground is located beside the national park office, across from the village of Songgye and close to the main trailhead of Yeong-bong. Although it looks like a big parking lot and lacks in the way of character, users have easy access to the park's amenities, which include a bus terminal (actually a parking lot between a gas station and store), banking machine, and post office. In addition, this campground has a lovely panoramic view of the mountain peaks. The washrooms are large and clean, with good ramps for wheelchair access. Electric units are installed throughout the campground. This campground speaks to campers who want convenience.

Songgye
Auto Campground
송계 자동차야영장

⌂ 1172-1 Songgye-ri, Hansu-myeon, Jecheon-si, Chungcheongbuk-do
℡ 043-653-3250
⊙ Open all year round

Transport Info   See Datdonjae Campground.

Buses depart from Chungju. Bus No. 222 goes to Songgye Campground five times daily; catch it outside of Chungju Bus Terminal by the taxi stand. Other buses depart for Songgye Valley from Jecheon (six times daily) and East Seoul (nine times daily).

Yongha
Campground
용하 야영장

⌂ 123-1 Worak-ri, Deoksan-myeon,
   Jecheon-si, Chungcheongbuk-do
✆ 043-653-3257
☉ Open all year round

Yongha Campground is about 2 km from the village of Eoksu 억수 (also spelled as Ak-su) along tranquil Yongha Valley 용하계곡. Although this campground is difficult to reach, there is something to be said for the stillness of the area. An early morning walk or bike ride can start your day on the right path. When they're in season, you can buy broccoli straight from the farmer's field or newly picked apples from the orchard along this valley road. Another, more beautiful trailhead for Yeong-bong is located 6 km from Eoksu. The trail starts at the base of the temple of Silleuk-sa 신륵사, with drinking water and chemical toilets available here. Campers who require information can visit the ranger station on the Silleuk-sa road.

The campground has one toilet block and one field kitchen. During the summer months, the on-site convenience store sells packaged noodles, snacks, and charcoal for barbecues. Campers should pack their own food and bring a head net—in the humid months of July and August, this area is plagued with pesky flies. There are a few *minbaks* in the area and two family operated stores in Eoksu that sell snack foods.

Transport Info a) From Jungbu Inland Expressway 45, take Exit 21 (Geosan Interchange) and follow Route 19 onto Route 3 going south toward Suanbo. Drive for one kilometer before turning left onto Route 36. Drive until you come to the T-intersection where Route 36 and Regional Road 597 meet. Continue for 4.8 km past the T-intersection along Route 36. Turn right at the national park sign, which reads "Worak-san 4.7 km, Silleuk-sa 6.3 km." This nice two-lane road follows the valley's river bed to another T-intersection. Turn right over the bridge and make the first left turn going to Yongha Valley. The campground is about 6 km beyond.

b) From Jungang Expressway 55, take Exit 26 (Danyang Interchange) and follow Route 5 going north. Turn left onto Route 36 and follow it to the other side of the park. Turn left onto Regional Road 534. Follow the road signs to Worak-san National Park and Yongha Valley. On the other side of the mountain, you will come to a sign reading "Yongha Gyegok Valley." Turn left at the sign. The campground is about 6 km beyond.

 Buses depart from the village of Deoksan 덕산 for Eoksu two times daily at 8:30 am and 5:30 pm. Campers who find this bus schedule inconvenient can take a fifteen-minute taxi ride over the mountain to the campground. Buses for Deoksan depart from Chungju (eight times daily), Jecheon (eight times daily), and Danyang (nine times daily).

See Datdonjae Campground.

Autumn scenery, Worak-san National Park

Songni-san
National Park

속리산 국립공원

Highlights

1. Hike to any one of the mountain peaks. At the summit are **impressive scenic views**.

2. Visit the ancient temple of **Beopju-sa** 법주사, with its striking bronze Buddha and historic relics.

3. Visit **hermitages** situated in the crevasses of the mountains. More often than not, it's a lofty hike to these places of solitude.

4. Saunter along the charming streets of the locally owned **tourist village of Sanae-ri** 사내리 and stroll by the village park river. This makes for a lovely evening walk to finish off a long day.

5. Check out the graceful 600-year-old pine tree named **Jeongipumsong** 정이품송.

Munjangdae summit (1,054m), Songni-san National Park

Located in the heart of central Korean farm country, Songni-san National Park is considered one of the finest, with trails leading to Cheonwang-bong 천왕봉 at 1,057 m. But not all visitors flock to this national park to conquer summits.

Just outside the village of Sanae-ri 사내리 is the sixth century Buddhist temple Beopju-sa 법주사. It's one of the largest and most beautiful temples surrounded by forest and mountains. Soaring over the grounds is a magnificent 33-meter bronze Buddha statue. This historic site is not to be missed!

When a great eighth century monk arrived in the area 233 years after Beopju-sa was built, even cows in the fields are said to have knelt down to receive him. The farmers in the area were amazed to see that even the animals asked forgiveness for their sins. As a result of this sighting, many of the farmers shaved

Beopju-sa

their heads and became monks. From this legend comes the name "Songni," which means "leaving the mundane life."

No fast food restaurants line the streets of Sanae-ri—it's all locally owned business. This is a welcome sight for those who really want to experience authentic Korean cuisine. Visitors might even find a souvenir or two as they saunter up and down the main street.

This national park has two campgrounds: Sanae-ri 사내리 and Hwayang-dong 화양동. Sanae-ri is privately operated, while Hwayang-dong is run by the Korea National Park Service.

Beopju-sa (043-544-5656, www.beopjusa.or.kr)

How to get to Beopju-sa and Sanae-ri Camp

From Expressway 30 (this route passes the town of Boeun 보은), take Exit 21 (Songni-san Interchange) and follow the road signs to Songni-san and Beopju-sa along Route 25. Turn onto Route 37 and drive over the mountain. Signage is clearly posted.

Buses depart 24 times daily from Cheongju Intercity Bus Terminal. The terminal is located across from Cheongju Express Bus Terminal. Other buses depart for Songni-san (Beopju-sa) from Seoul, Daejeon, and Suwon .

Sanae-ri Campground is tucked away in the back corner of Sanae-ri, about 700 m from the bus terminal. To find this campground, go along the main street toward Beopju-sa. Just before the post office, police station, and fire station (on the same side of the street), turn right onto an unlikely looking road that curves its way along a tree-lined walking path.

Hwayang-dong
Auto Campground
화양동 자동차야영장

⌂ 492 Huyeong-ri, Cheongcheon-myeon,
  Goesan-gun, Chungcheongbuk-do
☎ 043-832-4347
⊕ Open all year round

⬥ 75+	🚹 ✓	🚻 ✓	♿ ✓	🧑‍🦽 ✓	🚼	🚿
🚰 ✓	🔥 ✓	🛏	🍴 ✓	🪑	ℹ ✓	

There are lots of things to do at this popular riverside park, from river tubing to walking along a beautiful 4.5-kilometer paved path through Hwayang Valley 화양계곡. Accessible from this valley path are two hiking trails leading to the summit of Domyeong-san 도명산 (649 m). This region is pollution-free, and the back village roads are good for exploring by bicycle.

Located 500 m from the bus stop, this beautifully shaded campground has a hard dirt surface with grassy patches; fine gravel can be found on the upper level. There are four water stations, one portable toilet trailer, and two fixed bathroom blocks. On site is a 24-hour store that sells firewood, electricity use, and snack foods. The park ranger station is about 1.5 km from the campground at the head of the Hwayang Valley walking path. During the busier months (April, May, July, August, October, and November), campers can anticipate a lot of noise, as the tents are just meters apart from one another.

This campground lies between Expressways 35 and 45 deep inside rural territory in the northwest district of the national park. Located on Regional Road 32 in Hwayang Valley, it is south of Goesan 괴산, east of Cheongju 청주, and west of Mungyeong 문경. The campground is accessible from various regional routes; travelers should consult a good road atlas.

Access from the South

a) Follow the driving route to Sanae-ri, but veer left past Beopju-sa turn off, and continue along Route 37 heading north all the way to Cheongcheon 청천. There, you will turn right and follow the road sign to Chungju and Goesan. Drive for 2.6 km to Regional Road 32. Follow the brown and white signs along Regional Road 32 to Hwayang Valley. Signage is clearly posted. The campground is about a 45-minute drive north of Sanae-ri.

b) From Expressway 30, take exit 22 (Hwaseo Interchange) and follow Regional Road 49 to the north end of the park. When you come to the small village of Songmyeon-ri 송면리, where Regional Road 49 crosses Regional Road 517 and 32, veer left onto Regional Road 32 and follow it 7.7 kilometers. Follow the brown and white signs to Hwayang Valley. The road to the campground comes just before a small village bridge.

Access from the North

a) Take Route 19 heading south of Goesan. Drive for about one kilometer and turn left onto scenic Regional Road 49. At the T-intersection where Regional Roads 32 and 49 meet, turn right and drive 7.7 km along Regional Road 32. Follow the brown and white signs to Hwayang Valley.

b) Take Route 19 south of Goesan to Route 37. Where the two routes meet, follow the road sign to Songni-san and Cheongcheon. Drive along Route 37 until you come to a T-intersection. Turn left onto Regional Road 32. Follow the brown and white signs to Hwayang Valley. The campground is just after the second bridge crossing.

Buses depart for Hwayang Valley from Cheongju Intercity Bus Terminal (eight times daily) and Cheongcheon (three times daily).

The nearest train station is Cheongju Station, which is located 5 km from the bus terminals.

Gyeryong-san
National Park

계룡산 국립공원

Highlights

1. Visit the ancient Buddhist temples of **Gap-sa** 갑사 and **Donghak-sa** 동학사. Near Gap-sa, many hermitages sit on the mountainsides.

2. Treat yourself to a **seafood pancake** and beer. The food stalls along the riverside near Donghak-sa will welcome your patronage.

3. Spend a day in **Daejeon** 대전, the fifth largest city in Korea.

4. Climb along the **Nature Wall** 자연성능 ridge trail. This course is both challenging and stunning, with its many stairs and ladders hugging the contours of the mountain.

Gyeryong-san ridge at daybreak

If hiking is your sport, then Gyeryong-san National Park is the place to visit. The Nature Wall 자연성능 ridge trail from Gwaneum-bong 관음봉 to Sambul-bong 삼불봉 is quite literally breathtaking, at 800 m above sea level! Hikers on this course should pray for clear skies to maximize the scenic views and endure the four- to five-hour hiking course. This trail is not for the weak or fainthearted. It is no wonder that the park receives over a million trekkers a year. And although Gyeryong-san is smaller than most national parks, there is a multitude of other hiking trails, as well as two cultural properties within the park boundaries.

Donghak-sa 동학사 and Gap-sa 갑사 (one of Korea's most celebrated temples) are seperated by the Nature Wall mountain ridge. Both temples are set amid a serene landscape of forest and stream. Donghak-sa dates back to the year 724, when it served as a hermitage. The temple buildings underwent a turbulent history of construction, fire, and reconstruction over the last several centuries, with the last bout of destruction coming during the Korean War (1950–53). Today, Donghak-sa is known as one of Korea's largest Buddhist nunneries for trained and ordained female monks.

Although monks are considered pacifists today, this was not always the case. During the Japanese invasion of the 1590s, soldier-monks with training in the martial arts were called upon to defend their country. Fortifications had temples

attached to them. In Gap-sa hang portraits of three high priests, Yeonggyu, Samyeong, and Seosan—a testament to Buddhist history. These individuals served as warrior-monks in the Japanese war from 1592 to 1598. Other cultural assets at Gap-sa include its paintings, a bronze bell, a stone pagoda, a flagpole, and a shrine, among other artifacts.

Gyeryong-san National Park is central to three cities: Daejeon 대전, Gongju 공주, and Nonsan 논산. Buses travel from all three to various locations within the national park. Daejeon, Korea's fifth largest city and provincial capital of Chungcheongnam-do, is at the crossroads of rail and highway links, making it a terrific base for exploring the outer communities of central Korea, including the area's mountains and temples and the nearby cities of Gongju and Buyeo 부여. For those wanting to sightsee in Daejeon, the neighborhood of Yuseong 유성 has upscale shopping with lots of eateries, a foot spa, and hot spring resorts. These sights are easily accessible from the national park campground—take bus No. 107 to Yuseong Spa 유성온천 Subway Station. Should visitors wish to explore other parts of the city, they can board the metro train here. In 1993, Daejeon played host to the World Expo, the site for which has now been converted into a science park with the new name of Expo Science Park 엑스포과학공원. Maps and detailed locations are available at tourist information centers.

Gap-sa (043-857-8981, www.gapsa.org)

Donghak-sa
Campground
동학사 야영장

⌂ San 19 Hakbong-ri, Banpo-myeon,
   Gongju-si, Chungcheongnam-do
☎ 042-825-3005
⏱ Open all year round

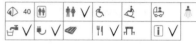

First impressions of this campground tend not to be favorable. The two bathroom blocks are worn down, and the forty designated campsites are too close to each other for comfort. Cut into a hillside are eight small graveled platforms, each having one electric box (eight outlets per box) and five designated campsites. This small campground maximizes its space, with the result that one tent door opens onto another. That said, the location of this campground is superb. The campground is conveniently located near the bus station in the Donghak-sa district. It is situated 150 m across from the parking lot and another 100 m up the hill. It is close to hiking trails, the temple of Donghak-sa, and the city Daejeon for those interested in day outings. The visitor center is on the other side of the ticket booth, toward Donghak-sa. Because weekend camping is popular here from spring to autumn, campers are advised to arrive early Saturday morning if they want to secure a site.

Transport Info From Expressway 251 (west side of Daejeon Circle Highway), take Exit 5 (Yuseong Interchange) and follow Route 32 onto Route 1. Follow the road signs to Gyeryong-san National Park and Donghak-sa.

 Buses depart for Donghak-sa from Daejeon Station. Bus No. 107 departs every 20 minutes, stopping at Yuseong Spa Subway Station (Exit 5) en route. From Daejeon Express Bus Terminal, take bus No. 102 or 106 to Yuseong Spa Station (Exit 6) and transfer onto 107. The Kumho Bus Terminal is within walking distance of Yuseong Spa Station.

 The nearest train station is Daejeon Station, which services regular and KTX trains.

A Buddhist nun at Donghak-sa.

Taean-haean
National Park
태안해안 국립공원

Highlights

1. Take long, leisurely strolls along a **white sand beach**, or go for an ocean dip.

2. Walk out to the mud flats with a pail and pick to do your own **clam digging**— cook your catch over a fire.

3. On the **salt farm flats** near Gomseom Beach 곰섬해변, watch farmers rake up crystal sea salt. Some farmers sell their product to the public.

4. Baeksajang-hang 백사장항 is home to many interesting seafood displays. Buy shellfish by the kilogram, or sit down at one of the many seafood restaurants by the port.

5. Take an hour-long ferry ride from **Yeongmok-hang** 영목항 to **Godae-do** 고대도 or **Janggo-do** 장고도 to explore small and simple island communities.

6. Capture one of the **stunning sunset views** along the west coast beaches— best from October to November, when the orb of the pink sun descends into the ocean.

Kkotji Beach with Grandmother and Grandfather Rocks in the distance, Taean-haean National Park

Taean-haean National Park protects a shoreline stretching for 230 km, with fine sand beaches measuring up to 1,500 m in width and up to 5 km in length. The entire protected area includes shoreline, islands, and sea. With the 30 beaches and diverse sea life, residents of the area make their livelihood from the tourist industry and fishing. This area is known for its shellfish, prawns, blue crabs, oysters, and sea bass.

The norm inside the national park is a mixture of restaurants and motel accommodations located among beach campgrounds—during peak season, the area gets rather noisy with beach parties and firecrackers going off during late night hours. If travelers are looking for peace and quiet, then the beaches of Duyeo 두여, Anmyeon 안면, and Gurye-po 구례포 are better choices. They are located slightly farther away from public buildings, and their sand quality remains clean.

If travelers are looking for activity—in and around the town of Anmyeon, there are singing rooms (called *noraebang* 노래방), shops, saunas, kiddie theme rides, lots of affordable motels, higher-end condominium resorts (one with an outdoor swimming pool), seafood eateries, and, along the Kkotji beachfront 꽃지해변, a lovely paved walking path.

The parks department claims that camping is permitted at almost all beach sites for a limited time from mid-June to mid-September. This section lists two types of campground: the Korea National Park Service site and, for the traveler's convenience, eight clean and orderly beach campgrounds that are run by their local community. The two types operate under different fee systems. Some of these beach campgrounds have more than one private operator, but all of the campgrounds listed are places where clearly posted signs state that "camping is permitted in designated areas."

Fortunately, there is little visual evidence left of the 2007 oil tanker spill that hit this area's northwest coast. This is probably due to the endless hours of hard work contributed to the cleanup effort by thousands of civilian volunteers, law enforcement workers, and military personnel, as well as the timely manner in which this disaster was handled.

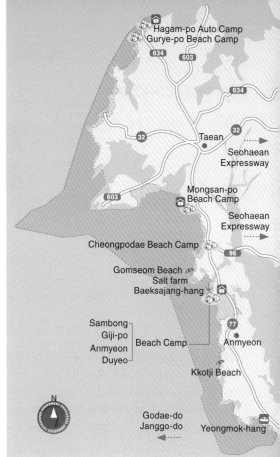

How to get to Taean From Seohaean Expressway 15

a) Take Exit 23 (Seosan Interchange) and follow Route 32 going west through Seosan 서산 to Taean. (Note: Traffic along this route is especially busy on weekend afternoons.)

b) Take Exit 22 (Haemi Interchange) and follow Route 29 to Route 32 through Seosan to Taean.

c) Take Exit 21 (Hongseong Interchange) and turn left onto Route 29. Then turn left again onto Regional Road 96. Drive to the near end and turn right onto Route 77 (going north to Taean).

All campgrounds are easily accessible by public transit from Taean Bus Terminal. The names of the beaches are clearly marked on bay signs in the terminal. Visitors should tell the bus driver which campground they want—otherwise, the driver might not stop. Campers should also anticipate short to long walks from the bus stop to their beach destination, as bus stops are not always located in front of the campground.

Hagam-po
Auto Campground
학암포 자동차야영장

⌂ 515-79 Bangal-ri, Wonbuk-myeon,
   Taean-gun, Chungcheongnam-do
☎ 041-674-3224
⊕ Open all year round

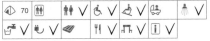

In this park, Hagam-po is the only campground operated by Korea National Park Service. There is still no other auto campground in the country that has the same quality of facilities as this camping site—it has sleek, modern stainless steel indoor kitchens, clean showers and restrooms, electricity, and picnic tables on four designated sites. This park is designed for those who don't want to rough

it. Furthermore, it has low curbs and a paved road, which speaks specifically to wheelchair accessibility. The price here is slightly elevated (9,000–11,000 won), but this is justifiable, since hot water is supplied. On the down side, the camping sites are small in size, and the campground gets crowded during peak season, which runs from April to November. All sites are reserved online or by phone. There is a ranger station on the grounds, and the village is located 100 m beyond the station, along with two beach coves.

Transport Info Travelers should drive to where Route 77 crosses over Route 32. Those coming westbound from Route 32 should take the exit ramp onto Route 77 and turn right. If you're coming northbound along Route 77, stay on it. Hagam-po Auto Campground is located about 20 km north of Taean in the village of Hagam-po (also spelled as Hakam-po). At the top of the exit ramp (on the bridge where Routes 32 and 77 cross), drive northbound 500 m to the intersection (entering Taean). Turn left at the intersection and follow the road signs to Hagam-po along Regional Road 603. The signage at the rotary is confusing, so take it slow. Drive for several kilometers along Regional Road 603 before making a left turn onto Regional Road 634.

TIP

What to do when there aren't any auto camping spots?

Instead of turning right for Hagam-po Auto Campground, take a left onto the single-lane road. A privately operated campground is only a few hundred meters away. Tents here are pitched along the beachfront or in the cluster of trees on the hillside. Because the terrain is soft sand, users should pin down their tent in case of strong winds or rain. There are two on-site bathroom blocks equipped with a baby changing table, and shower room. Food and water are easily accessible in town.

| Locally Operated Campgrounds |

☉ Mid-June to mid-September (except for Mongsan-po, which is open all year round).
▱ Rates vary from campground to campground and are based on the services offered.

Gurye-po Beach Campground 구례포 해수욕장

⌂ Hwangchon-ri, Wonbuk-myeon, Taean-gun, Chungcheongnam-do

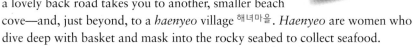

If it's solitude you want, then this is the campground to
visit, especially during June or September (before and
after the busy summer season). Four things make this
spot unique. First, the quality of sand is clean. Second,
the park is set off from the main road and slightly
isolated. Third, it is less commercial, since there are no
major hotels or motels surrounding the park. And finally,
a lovely back road takes you to another, smaller beach
cove—and, just beyond, to a *haenyeo* village 해녀마을. *Haenyeo* are women who
dive deep with basket and mask into the rocky seabed to collect seafood.

Gurye-po Beach is a small, intimate cove that stretches for about 500 m. The
campground is situated in a large pine forest behind the dunes. From the main
road, there are three entrances leading to the campground and beach. Along the
beach are two bathroom blocks that inevitably get gritty from users tracking
in sand. The restaurants and stores in the immediate area are seasonal, so it is
recommended that you pack water and food for this location.

🚗 See Hagam-po Auto Campground. Gurye-po is located 1.5 km before the village of Hagam-po.

Cheongpodae Beach Campground 청포대 해수욕장

⌂ Woncheong-ri, Nam-myeon, Taean-gun, Chungcheongnam-do

This park won't get any awards for design, with its flat and square sandy parcels
of land located on either side of a newly renovated bathroom block. It is,
however, situated on a long, wide stretch of really nice beach! Sunset strolls are
highly recommended. Those so inclined can walk along the beach to Mongsan-
po, which is located a few kilometers away. This campground is a ten-minute
walk from the bus stop on Route 77.

🚗 See Mongsan-po Campground on p. 79.

Mongsan-po Beach Campground 몽산포 해수욕장

⌂ Sinjang-ri, Nam-myeon, Taean-gun, Chungcheongnam-do

Mongsan-po is the largest and most popular campground in Taean-haean National Park. Set among restaurants, rental cabins, pension houses, motels and *minbaks*, this auto and forested campground can accommodate hundreds of tents. It's popular among families and large groups of people, who come to picnic, play, and relax.

This campground is divided into sections. The most popular one is central to all the facilities and allows campers to park their car beside their tent. It gets quieter as you move away from the hub—travelers looking for solitude should camp in the forested area at the north end. Mongsan-po is located behind a nice long and wide stretch of beach, which faces westward and gets lovely sunset views.

The bathroom facilities at the campground include newly constructed buildings alongside older portable ones. The campground terrain is flat, and tent pads are shaded by a large pine forest. A ranger station is located at the park gate.

🚗 From Seohaean Expressway 15, take Exit 21 (Hongseong Interchange) and turn left onto Route 29. Turn left again onto Regional Road 96 and follow it to the near end. Turn right onto Route 77 and follow the road signs to Mongsan-po and Cheongpodae. These two campgrounds are about 5 km apart from each other.

A family relaxes on the beach of Taean-haean National Park

Sambong Beach Campground 삼봉 해수욕장

⌂ Changgi-ri, Anmyeon-eup, Taean-gun, Chungcheongnam-do

Sambong is the first of four campgrounds on a beautiful, wide stretch of beach that is about 5 km long. This large forested campground is long and narrow and has a picturesque wooded trail through the center of the park, which leads to Gigi-po Beach boardwalk about a kilometer farther on. The tent pads are positioned among trees on a small hillside, sandwiched between the beach and trail. This campground has three field kitchens, one toilet trailer, two shower buildings, and two fixed bathroom blocks. There is a ranger station on site, as well as several restaurants in close proximity to the campground.

 From Seohaean Expressway 15, take Exit 21 (Hongseong Interchange) and turn left onto Route 29. Take another left onto Regional Road 96 and follow it to the near end. Turn left onto Route 77 going south. Drive for a short distance and turn right onto Baeksajang 1-gil. A road sign will announce Baeksajang 백사장—drive 300 m and turn left onto Haeangwangwang-ro 해안관광로. Located along this road are four campgrounds: Sambong, Giji-po, Anmyeon, and Duyeo. Brown and white signs will direct you to your beach choice.

Giji-po Beach Campground 기지포 해수욕장

⌂ Changgi-ri, Anmyeon-eup, Taean-gun, Chungcheongnam-do

This simple beach park is scenic, with its grassy sand dunes and wheelchair-accessible boardwalk trail. The trail leads to the village of Sambong and a ranger station about a kilometer away. Giji-po has a newly constructed parking lot, visitor center, and bathroom block. Tents are pitched in the soft, sandy pine forest just behind the dunes. Pack water and food for this location.

 See Sambong Campground.

Anmyeon Beach Campground 안면 해수욕장

 Jeongdang-ri, Anmyeon-eup, Taean-gun, Chungcheongnam-do

"Unspoiled" is the best word to describe this small park. Even the public washroom is located 50 m across the street so as not to disturb the natural terrain. Hopefully, the parks department will recognize its natural beauty and prohibit development close to the water's edge. This campground is located on a nice long stretch of beach extending from Sambong to Duryeo. Tents are pitched in the small pine forest behind the dunes on either side of the beach entrance. Campers must park in the parking lot and carry their gear onto the site.

See Sambong Campground.

Duyeo Beach Campground 두여 해수욕장

 Jeongdang-ri, Anmyeon-eup, Taean-gun, Chungcheongnam-do

There are two small flat sandy areas set aside for this campground. One is on the left of the parking lot, the other on the right. Thankfully, a new toilet trailer in the parking lot has replaced the old pit toilets, and much care has gone into cleaning up this spot. With only toilet services available, this campground is located in a scenic and isolated place at the end of a nice long stretch of beach. From this campground, a trailhead leads to an observation site 500 m away.

See Sambong Campground.

NORTHEAST

GANGWON-DO

Seorak-san National Park

Odae-san National Park

Chiak-san National Park

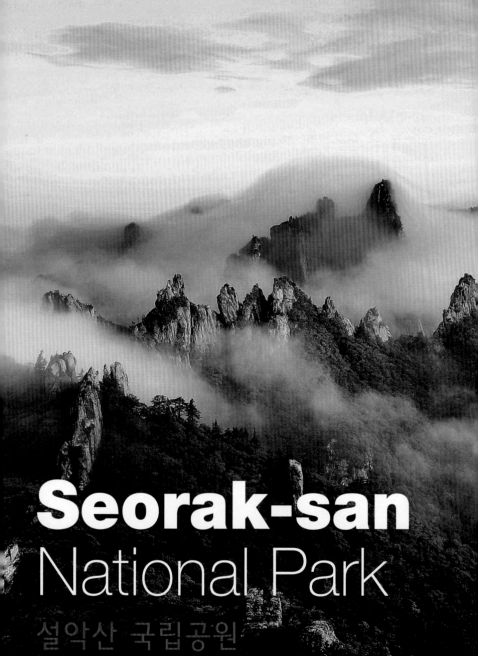

Seorak-san
National Park
설악산 국립공원

Highlights

1. Be among the thousands of tourists who visit Seorak-san around mid-October to see the **changing colors of fall foliage**.

2. **Ulsan-bawi** 울산바위 **trail** has a vertical steel ladder attached to the bare rock face. This landscape architecture takes hikers to a place where they normally would not have access.

3. Take the cable car to the **Gwongeum Fortress** 권금성 ruins for a fantastic view.

4. Get a first-hand glimpse of the **DMZ (Demilitarized Zone)**, where the **Unification Observatory** 통일전망대 stands overlooking the border between South and North Korea. Nearby is the **DMZ Museum** DMZ 박물관 with fascinating exhibits of the border region.

5. Seek out some of the country's **nicest beaches**, which run along the east coast.

6. Be adventurous and eat raw fish at the **Daepo-hang** 대포항 in **Sokcho** 속초.

7. Soak in **hot mineral spas** at a local resort, or have a fun-filled day at the **water theme park**.

The dramatic mountaintops of Seorak-san are the little Alps of Korea. Majestic granite peaks soar upward, attracting rock climbers, hikers, and those who just want to walk among beautiful forests and along river trails. The park boasts 28 steep peaks, with Daecheong-bong 대청봉 the highest at 1,708 m.

Seorak-san is divided into three regions: Outer Seorak 외설악, Inner Seorak 내설악 and South Seorak 남설악. Within the outer region are a number of interesting places to explore: walk through the ancient temple of Sinheung-sa 신흥사, or climb the harrowing steel case ladder on the rock

Soseung Waterfall

Snow-covered Cheonbuldong Valley

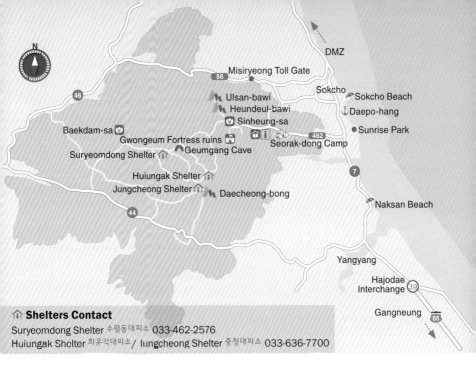

🏠 **Shelters Contact**
Suryeomdong Shelter 수렴동대피소 033-462-2576
Huiungak Shelter 희운각대피소 / Jungcheong Shelter 중청대피소 033-636-7700

face of Ulsan-bawi 울산바위. The views of the East Sea from the summit (873 m) are breathtaking and well worth the effort. You can also have your picture taken pushing the huge Heundeul-bawi 흔들바위 ("shaking rock"), which totters back and forth. Climb to Geumgang Cave 금강굴 and say a prayer, or ride the cable car to the Gwongeum Fortress 권금성 ruins at 800 m.

This park has a number of hidden gems, and park rangers at the visitor center (2 km from the campground) can provide campers with park maps, and shelter and trail information. The center also has Internet access, a museum, and a small theater that shows a video on the park. Please note that the visitor center is closed on Mondays. Other tourist information can be found at the Sunrise Park 해맞이공원 tourist center in the town of Sokcho 속초; it carries pamphlets and maps for the greater area.

The other two regions, Inner and South Seorak, are accessible from Regional Road 56 and Routes 44 and 46. The favored place where Seorak-san has been most often photographed is located just past the Misiryeong 미시령 toll gate on Regional Road 56. A huge parking lot was constructed for gawkers and photographers alike. The three connecting routes (44, 46, and 56) make for a lovely day drive. Travelers can visit the temple of Baekdam-sa 백담사, eat lunch along the way at one of the roadside or village restaurants, or approach a hiking trail from the quieter side of the park. Near the town of Yangyang 양양, the landscape changes from forested mountains to flat, fertile land. Residents in this area make their livelihood from farming and fishing. The flavor is different, but just as appealing.

😊 Sinheung-sa (033-636-7044, www.sinhungsa.or.kr)
   Baekdam-sa (033-462-5565, www.baekdamsa.org)

TIP

Biking in Sokcho

Rent a bike near **Expo Tower** 엑스포타워 on **Cheongcho-ho** 청초호 → **Follow the road under the bridge** → **Gaetbae ferry dock** 갯배 선착장 → **Seokbong Ceramic Museum** 석봉 도자기 미술관 → **Jungang Market** 중앙시장 → **Lighthouse Observatory** 등대전망대 → **Yeongnang-ho** 영랑호

Cheongcho-ho (left),
Expo Tower (right) and
Gaetbae ferry (bottom)

Seorak-dong
Campground
설악동 야영장

⌂ 370 Seorak-dong, Sokcho-si,
Gangwon-doo
✆ 033-636-1262
◔ Open all year round

◁⟩ 300+	👫		👫 ✓	♿ ✓	🤿 ✓	🛒 ✓	🚿 ✓
🗑 ✓	🔌 ✓	🧹	🍴 ✓	🎋	ⓘ ✓		

Seorak-dong Campground is located on Regional Road 462, halfway between the park gate and coastal Route 7. "Impressive" is the best adjective to describe this campground: it is clean beyond measure, well-organized, conveniently located, and easily accessible. The facilities on site include four toilet blocks, three or four shower buildings and field kitchens, a sports ground, and a convenience store. The design of the campground allows campers to park their car alongside their tent. Campers should be aware that space is limited on weekends in the month of August. The park claims that this campground can accommodate up to 400 tents, but given the actual size of the large tents and eating shelters usually pitched at this park, Seorak-dong realistically has land capacity for about 300 tents.

Transport Info From Donghae Expressway 65, take Exit 39 (Hajodae Interchange) and follow the road signs along Route 7 going north to Sokcho. The road opposite Sunrise Park (Regional Road 462) goes into the heart of Seorak-san, where the campground is located. (Note: Donghae Expressway 65 is currently under construction to extend its route farther north. New highway exits are expected to open.)

🚌 Two local buses, No. 7 and 7-1, depart for Seorak-san National Park from Sokcho every fifteen minutes. They can be boarded outside the intercity bus terminal or at the bus stop across from Sokcho Express Bus Terminal. They go past the campground and turn around at the park gate. Tell the bus driver you want to get off at the campground, or else the driver might not stop.

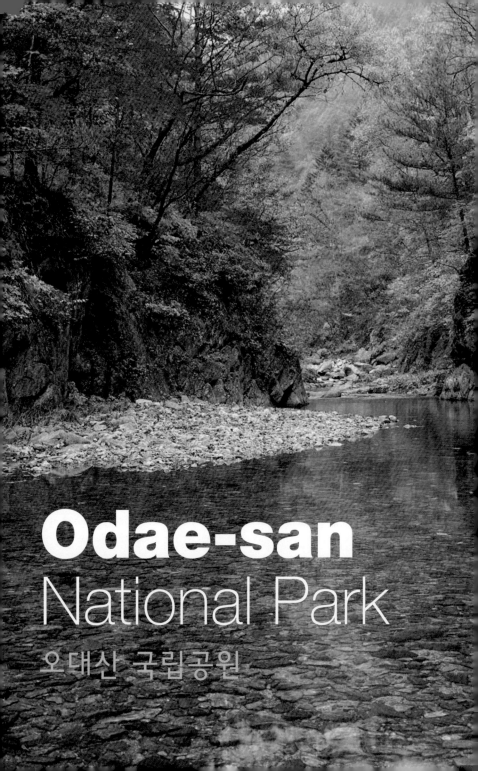

Odae-san
National Park
오대산 국립공원

Highlights

1. Take an early morning walk along the river road between the temples of **Woljeong-sa** 월정사 and **Sangwon-sa** 상원사 as the sun rises over the crest of the mountains.

2. Bypass Yeongdong Expressway 50 and take the more scenic Route 6 over **Jingogae Pass** 진고개. This road positively snakes its way into the valley below.

3. Detour into **Pyeongchang** 평창, which is famous for its **winter skiing** from November to March. In 2018, Pyeongchang will host the Winter Olympics .

4. Spend the day swimming in the ocean, or stroll along a **white sand beach**. Sogeumgang Campground is an easy drive from a number of public beaches.

5. Check out the city of **Gangneung** 강릉. The largest city in South Korea's northeast, it boasts beaches and historical properties.

As the legend goes, a Silla-era monk by the name of Jajang Yulsa traveled to China to study. Upon his return, he thought that one of the mountains resembled China's Mt. Wutai ("Odae" in Korean)—hence, the name of this mountain region.

At first sight, Odae-san does not have the dramatic jagged and bare-faced granite peaks of nearby Seorak-san National Park, nor does it have the same level of tourist appeal. Closer inspection, however, shows that this national park has its own unique and peaceful qualities. Deep in the woods stand two high-ranking temples, Woljeong-sa 월정사 and Sangwon-sa 상원사. The road to Sangwon-sa is paved only halfway, leaving the traveler to maneuver around the potholes in the hard dirt. Both temples are serviced by local buses from Jinbu진부.

The peak of Biro-bong 비로봉 (1,563 m) is easily accessible from Sangwon-sa. An extensive hike in a horseshoe formation will take the hiker to Dongdae-san 동대산 (1,433 m) and down the mountainside back onto the dirt road, or farther on to Jingogae Pass 진고개.

In the Woljeong-sa district, Route 6 forks east of Odae-san National Park Office. This beautiful scenic road snakes its way over the mountains to the other side, where Sogeumgang Auto Campground 소금강 자동차야영장 is situated and other trails begin or end. Due to budget constraints and environmental protection efforts, Odae-san National Park now operates only one campground.

Woljeong-sa (033-339-6606~7, www.woljeongsa.org)

On the road to Woljeong-sa (top), Family camping in Sogeumgang (bottom)

Sogeumgang
Auto Campground
소금강 자동차야영장

⌂ 58 Samsan-ri, Yeongok-myeon,
   Gangneung-si, Gangwon-do
ℱ 033-661-4161
⊕ Open all year round

◁》 100+ 👫	👫 ✓	♿ ✓	🧺 ✓	🚲	🚿 ✓
🚰 ✓	♨	◢	🍴 ✓	⛩	ⓘ ✓

Unique to this campground are the nine sites allotted for camping vans; the rest of the campground is designated for tents. This campground has five water stations, three toilet blocks, and one shower building. During the colder months, the toilet blocks are closed, and campers must cross over the bridge to use the public facilities in the tourist village about 150 m away. This is a typical-looking auto campground built in an open space without a lot of privacy. The bonus is its close proximity to ocean beaches. For those wanting to hike mountains, maps and trail information can be found at the ranger station 500 m from the campground.

Transport Info From Donghae Expressway 65, take Exit 37 (Bukgangneung Interchange) and follow coastal Route 7 going north toward Jumunjin 주문진. Turn onto Route 6 going west toward Jinbu and follow the signs to Odae-san National Park and Sogeumgang.

🚌 Bus No. 303 departs thirteen times daily for Sogeumgang from Gangneung's express and intercity bus terminals. The bus stop is in front of both terminals which stand next to each other.

🚆 The nearest train station is Gangneung Station. The bus stop for bus No. 303 is 270 m around the corner from the station.

Chiak-san
National Park

치악산 국립공원

Highlights

1. Hike the trail between the peaks of **Biro-bong** 비로봉 and **Namdae-bong** 남대봉.

2. Explore the temple of **Guryong-sa** 구룡사 and see its famous four guardians of the heavenly kings. Buddhists come from far and wide to pray at this sacred place.

3. Climb up to and follow along the ruins of **Yeongwon Mountain Fortress** 영원산성 in Geumdae Valley 금대계곡. Imagine what an arduous effort it was to collect, lift, and transport the stones to build such a wall along the mountain ridge.

4. Enjoy the **distant sounds of meditation** from Guryong-sa while camping 200 m away at **Daegok Campground** 대곡 야영장. The campground's isolation and lack of vehicle access make this spot a gem.

5. Chiak-san's regional district is noted for growing potatoes. Food stalls located just outside the park gate near Guryong-sa sell affordable and delicious **potato pancakes** 감자전.

Sangwon-sa sits at over 1,000 m above sea level

A traveler, it is said, was walking along a narrow path on his way to take the state examination when he came across a pheasant wrapped in the coils of a serpent. Feeling sympathy for the pheasant, he rescued it by killing the coiled creature. After sundown, the traveler was in search of a place to stay for the night to rest his weary body. A kind woman offered her hospitality. He accepted, but to his surprise, during the night she turned herself into a serpent and encircled the traveler. She was the wife of the slain snake, now taking her revenge. The only way the traveler could be saved, she told him, was if the bell at the temple of Sangwon-sa 상원사 rang three times before sunset. To repay his debt of gratitude, the pheasant sacrificed his life ringing the bell on his head. In the end, the traveler was saved. A picture depicting this legend still remains at Sangwon-sa. The *chi* in Chiak-san means "pheasant," and it is thought that the name of this national park originates from the legend.

Located near the city of Wonju 원주 in Gangwon-do, Chiak-san National Park lies snugly in the corner between the Yeongdong 50 and Jungang 55 Expressways. Although average in size, this park has the bonus of being largely untouched. The park boasts ten peaks rising up over 1,000 m, with Biro-bong 비로봉 to the north reaching 1,288 m and Namdae-bong 남대봉 to the south ascending to 1,185 m. A mountain ridge trail runs north-south between these peaks.

Less than a three-hour drive from Seoul, this park is situated halfway between the West and East Seas. Although not the busiest national park, it does get its fair share of visitors. Part of its popularity can be attributed to the temple of Guryong-sa 구룡사. Counted as one of the older higher-ranking Buddhist temples in Korea, it is located in a lovely forest along a picturesque walking path.

Chiak-san National Park is only accessible by four valley roads: Guryong 구룡계곡, Geumdae 금대계곡, Seongnam 성남계곡, and Bugok 부곡계곡. Situated in the valleys of Guryong and Geumdae are the park's three campgrounds, two of them auto campgrounds and the third a fifteen-minute walk-in.

Due to the park's popularity, Korea National Park Service is making great efforts to control car access. Three large parking lots have been constructed for those visiting by way of Guryong Valley. Visitors must park their car and walk to the gate entrance. In parking lot No. 2, not far from Guryong Auto Campground, there is a national park office with an information center.

🐢 Guryong-sa (033-732-4800, www.guryongsa.or.kr)

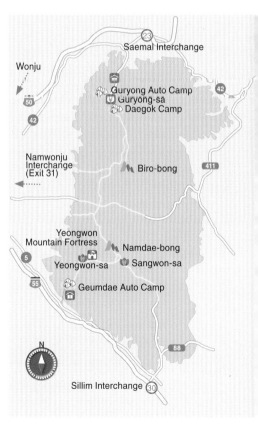

A picture depicting the legend hangs at Sangwon-sa.

Guryong Auto Campground
구룡 자동차야영장

⌂ 900 Hakgok-ri, Socho-myeon, Wonju-
   si, Gangwon-do
℡ 033-732-4635
⊙ Open all year round

Guryong is a typical-looking auto campground built in an open space with paved road and grassy gravel tent pads. The campground has 70 official campsites, with electric units on each site. There are three outdoor kitchens and three toilet blocks in operation during the warmer months, but in winter the flush facilities are locked up and replaced with a pit toilet trailer. For those campers planning to climb the peak of Biro-bong, Guryong is ideally located for an early morning start.

Transport Info From Yeongdong Expressway 50, take Exit 23 (Saemal Interchange) and turn right at the first T-intersection. At the next T-intersection, turn right again onto Route 42. Drive for about 2.4 km toward Wonju. Make a left turn into Guryong Valley and follow the national park signs. The campgrounds and parking lots are located at the end of the valley road.

 Buses No. 41 and 41-1 depart from Wonju Station for Guryong-sa. The bus stop is around the corner from the train station. The easiest way for travelers to get to the campground from Wonju's express and intercity bus terminals is to take a taxi to Wonju Station (about 3 km away).

 The nearest train station is Wonju Station (see By Bus).

This campground is located in a lovely pine forest just 200 m from the temple of Guryong-sa along a mountain creek. To get there, campers should follow the dirt walking trail past the temple, over the bridges, and around the crystal clear water pool. Daegok has two cleared sections of ground set up for tents, located about 100 m apart from each other. Each section has its own outdoor kitchen, but there is only one toilet block for the entire campground. The forest turns pitch black at night, and campers will need to see where they are stepping. Don't forget to pack a flashlight!

Daegok
Campground
대곡 야영장

🏠 1044-1 Hakgok-ri, Socho-myeon, Wonju-si, Gangwon-do
📞 033-731-1289
🕐 Officially June to August, but people camp from early spring to late autumn.

Transport Info See Guryong Auto Campground.

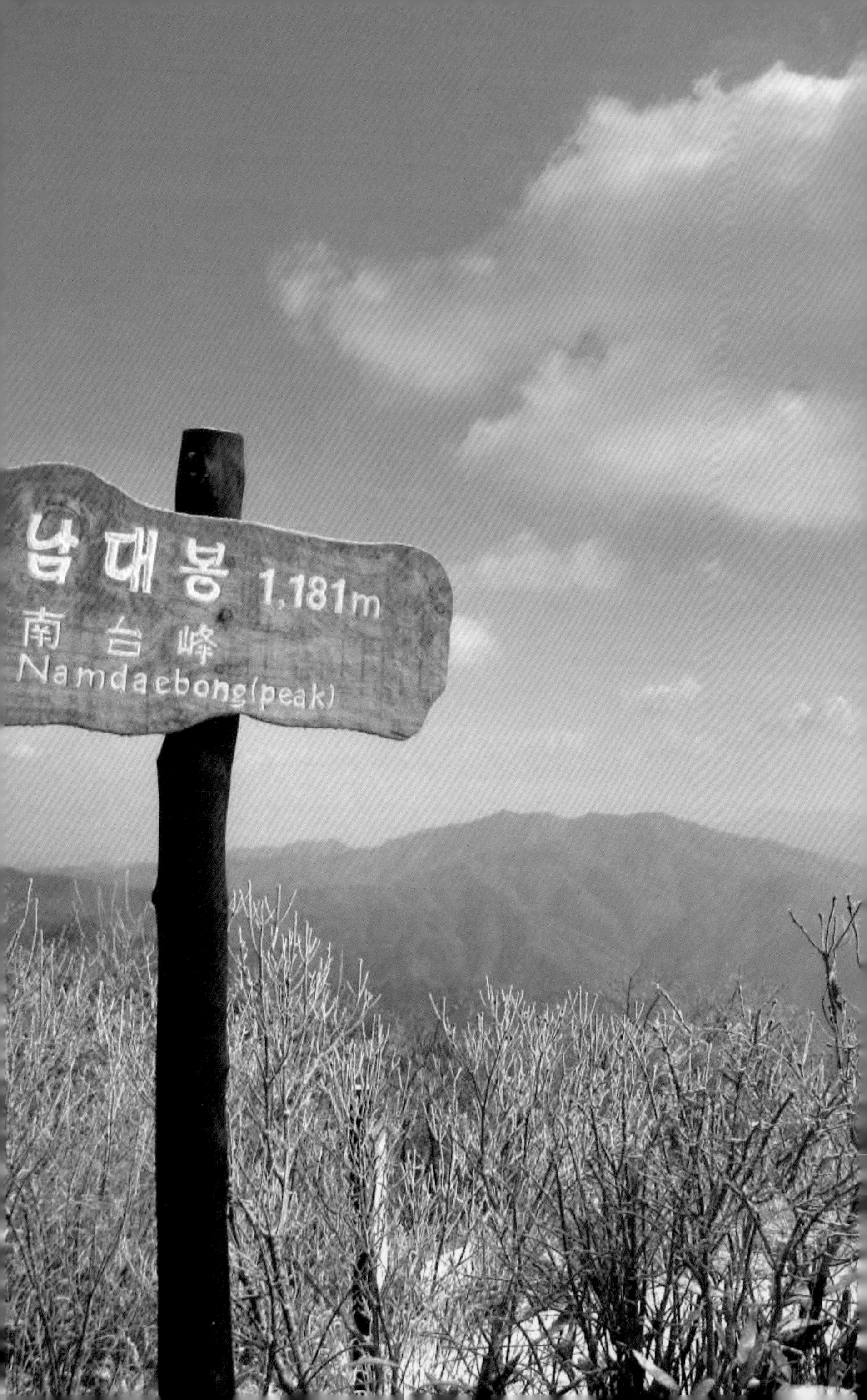
남대봉 1,181m
南台峰
Namdaebong(peak)

Geumdae Auto Campground
금대 자동차야영장

🏠 1333 Geumdae-ri, Panbu-myeon,
   Wonju-si, Gangwon-do
📞 033-763-5232
🕐 Open all year round

◁)) 49	🚻	👫 ✓	♿ ✓	🧺 ✓	🚌	🚿
🚰 ✓	🔥	〰	🍴 ✓	⛲ ✓	ⓘ ✓	

"Well organized" and "clean" are the best words to describe this campground. Cut into a hillside, the park has three tiers, with toilet facilities at the top and bottom. In the center of the park are communal picnic tables and a field kitchen. Geumdae Campground is ideally located for those who want to climb the peak of Namdae-bong or visit the two temples of Yeongwon-sa 영원사 and Sangwon-sa. For the adventurous is the climb up to the ruins of Yeongwon Mountain Fortress.

Unfortunately, there is no bus service along Geumdae Road, so campers using public transit will have to walk the distance (2.4 km from Route 5) or hail a cab.

Transport Info 🚗 From Jungang Expressway 55

a) Take Exit 30 (Sillim Interchange) and follow Route 5 north toward Wonju. Turn right at the road sign for Chiak-san and Geumdae Valley. Drive under the tall concrete railway bridge and follow the road to the very end. This pretty road starts as two lanes before eventually merging into one.

b) Take Exit 31 (Namwonju Interchange) and follow Route 19 onto Route 5 south through the city streets. (Note: Road signs along this route are more difficult to follow.) Drive south along Route 5 until you come to the road sign for Chiak-san and Geumdae Valley. Turn left there and drive to the end of the valley road.

 Buses (No. 21, 22, 23, 24, and 25) depart from Wonju Station for Geumdae Valley. The bus stop is located around the corner from the train station, which is about 3 km from the express and intercity bus terminals. From Sillim Station, take bus No. 21 or 22 for Geumdae. The bus stop is at the base of the hill. Do not cross the road.

 The nearest train stations are Wonju and Sillim Stations.

SOUTHEAST

GYEONGSANGBUK-DO | GYEONGSANGNAM-DO

Juwang-san National Park

Gyeongju National Park

Gaya-san National Park

Jiri-san National Park

Hallyeo-haesang National Park

Juwang-san
National Park
주왕산 국립공원

Highlights

1. Walk along the lovely forested path to the park's **three scenic waterfalls**. The first in particular has a canyon boardwalk attached to the rock face. This landscape architecture takes people into a space that they normally would not have access to.

2. Spend a day by the ocean. **Daejin Beach** 대진해변 is just an hour away.

3. Bike through quiet back roads among **fruit orchards** or the beautiful **Okgye Valley** 옥계계곡.

4. Hike to the Juwang-san summit and the peak of **Janggun-bong** 장군봉.

A part of the Taebaek Mountain Range, Juwang-san is prized for its unique rock formations and the temple of Daejeon-sa 대전사. The name of this National Park originates from the time when Prince Juwon of the Silla Dynasty stayed in the area to practice asceticism. Before this period, the area was referred to as Seokbyeong-san, or "stone screen mountain," because the rocks are aligned to form a shield.

Immersed in fruit orchard country, this gem of a national park offers a truly diverse range of activities. The quieter back roads are superb for exploring by bicycle, and if you visit during harvest time in mid-August, roadside stalls will be there to entice you with apples and peaches freshly picked from the tree. You can even smell the sweetness of the fruit in the air during harvest time.

The popular treks are to the Juwang-san summit (720 m) and the not-so-challenging Janggun-bong 장군봉 (686 m). Visitors who don't want to complete a four- to six-hour hiking course can make a return hike to a summit only. In particular, the short trek to Janggun-bong offers some scenic views of the area.

Just as rewarding, and equally popular, is the pretty trek along and through the vertical rock formations to the three picturesque waterfalls of Juwang Valley 주왕계곡. The first has a dramatic boardwalk hugging closely to the underside of a canyon rock wall, with gushing mountain water rushing snake-like through a narrow opening. With its micro-climate, this is a cooling place on a hot summer's day. But in the humid months of July and August, the forest is plagued with pesky flies, so bring a head net for protection during this time.

Just an hour away is Daejin Beach 대진해변, with its golden sand. This beach is at least 3 km long and makes for a great day outing. Whether it's a cool ocean dip, a bike ride through orchard country, a hike to a summit, or a walk to scenic waterfalls, each of these activities offers a great way to experience Korea.

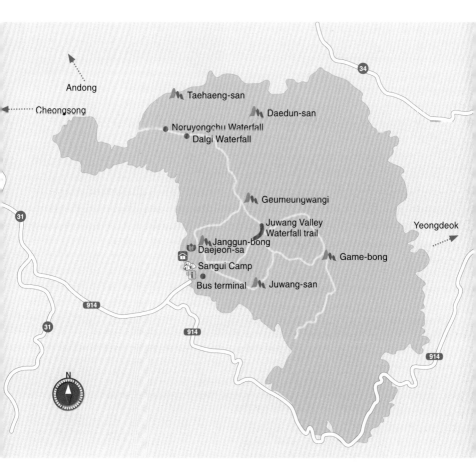

Sangui
Campground
상의 야영장

🏠 333-1 Sangui-ri, Budong-myeon,
   Cheongsong-gun, Gyeongsangbuk-do
📞 054-873-0014~5
🕐 Open all year round

This well-organized campground has paved roads leading to three tiers. Twelve sites on the top tier have electric units. While the two upper tiers have assigned campsite numbers with parking spaces, the lower level is flat ground, where campers pitch their tents randomly. Across from the campground are numerous restaurants, a park visitor center, and the park's bus station. Daejeon-sa is a ten-minute walk from the campground.

Transport Info This park has a distant location east of Andong 안동 on the lower east side of the Korean Peninsula, away from any major expressways. This means that there is a plethora of back road driving routes available to the traveler. The campground location is halfway between Cheongsong 청송 to the west and Yeongdeok 영덕 to the east. These two cities are linked by Regional Road 914, which runs south of the park. The campground is only accessible from this road. Clear road signage along Regional Road 914 will direct the traveler to Juwang-san National Park and Daejeon-sa, which lies within the park boundaries.

 Buses depart for Juwang-san from Cheongsong (20 times daily), Busan (two times daily), Daegu (three times daily), and Seoul (via Andong, six times daily). The national park bus terminal is located across from the campground.

1. Local bus stop   2. Freshly picked peaches   3. Canyon boardwalk   4. Jusanji Pond

Gyeongju
National Park

경주 국립공원

Highlights

1. Savor the moment as you walk through the beautiful **Bulguk-sa** 불국사, listed as historic and scenic site No. 1 for all of Korea.

2. Revel in the magnificent artistry of an 8th century Buddha carving, the **Seokguram Grott**o 석굴암.

3. Count the number of bricks it took to construct the 7th century **Cheomseongdae** 첨성대 astrological observatory. The base consists of twelve stones, each representing a month of the year. There are thirty layers, one for each day of the month, and 366 stones to represent each day of the year.

4. Walk or bike to the **Noseo-dong** 노서동 and **Nodong-dong** 노동동 tombs in the city center. A large number of huge grassy mounds stand erected as examples of royal burials. South of Nodong-dong is **Tumuli Park** 대릉원 where **Cheonmachong** 신바룡, the Heavenly Horse Tomb, has been cross-sectioned for public viewing.

5. Tour **Gyeongju National Museum** 국립경주박물관, where valuable treasures from the Silla era are on display.

6. Hike through **Nam-san** 남산. This small mountain abounds with historic relics from hermitages, pagodas, rock carvings, and so much more.

7. Taste the delicious **ssambap** 쌈밥 menu served throughout the Gyeongju area.

Bulguk-sa and its Dabo Pagoda, erected in the 8th century

Historians often refer to Gyeongju as a "museum without walls." Artifacts from a thousand-year Silla Dynasty (from 57 BC to 935 AD) are scattered throughout the general area. They rest on hillsides and stand along walkways. They are set in gardens, constructed in forests, and showcased in museums. The unearthing of these artifacts unlocked a story of life at a particular time when Gyeongju ruled as the Silla-era capital. The name "Gyeongju," however, was not given to the city until 940 AD. Prior to this time, the settlement was known by other names: Seorabeol (meaning "capital"), Gyerim ("rooster's forest"), and Geumseong ("city of gold").

The national park is divided into eight compact mountainous regions, each of them easily accessible by car, by public transit, and, in some areas, by bike and on foot. Envision the city of Gyeongju as the central point from which these eight districts radiate. To the south is the small, protected mountain region of Nam-san 남산. East stands the largest protected mountain region, Toham-san 토함산. Northeast of Gyeongju is the Sogeumgang 소금강 region; to the west lie the Hwarang 화랑, Seoak 서악, Gumi-san 구미산, and Danseok-san 단석산 regions.

These protected mountainous districts form a natural fort around the heart of Gyeongju. This might raise a question in some minds: was this natural fort

King Munmu's underwater tomb of the Silla Kingdom

Samneung Forest, Nam-san

formation a factor that allowed Gyeongju to remain the stronghold for centuries? Embedded within these regions are shrines, palace ruins, temples, Buddhist effigies, pleasure gardens, castles, rock carvings, and so much more. The eighth and final protected region, Daebon 대본, lies along the coast, overlooking a royal birthplace and tomb.

After the fall of Gyeongju in the 10th century, the region fell into forgotten bliss. It was raided, stripped, and ravaged over centuries by invading Mongols and Japanese; neglected by Korea's own dynasties; and finally colonized by Japan in 1910. The artifacts you see in Gyeongju today are largely the product of a cultural resurrection that began at the turn of the 20th century. The story of Seokguram Grotto 석굴암 is a prime example of this revival. The Buddha carving was accidentally rediscovered during the Japanese occupation, and although the Japanese would have gladly removed this beautifully crafted granite artifact to one of their own museums back home, there was local resistance, which led to the start of its repair in 1913. It wasn't until 1961, when UNESCO supported a more meticulous restoration, that Seokguram Grotto gained recognition as a national treasure. Even today, you can find ongoing excavations, restorations, and new discoveries in Gyeongju.

Anapji Pond, formely a royal pleasure garden

The Highlights section of this national park covers the more popular important sights. Time allotted to this national park will depend on the traveler's curiosity and schedule.

Gyeongju has two primary tourist information booths, one by the rail station and the other beside the express bus terminal. Friendly English-speaking staff can provide the traveler with maps, suggestions, orientation, and transport information. Near the tourist booth by the express bus station are bike rentals, should travelers wish to discover the heart of Gyeongju on two wheels. Tours are available, but not necessary. Gyeongju is tourist-friendly.

The downtown core of Gyeongju is not so different from other cities. It services the greater community, and its urban plan is grid-like. There are two bus terminals (express and inter-city), affordable motels that service the tourist industry, restaurants, supermarkets, and two train stations, one downtown and the other on the outskirts. An old building restriction forbidding high-rises in the heart of Gyeongju has forced the larger, more exclusive hotels to locate themselves several kilometers outside the city around Bomun-ho 보문호. This lake is also home to a small theme park.

Bulguksa (054-746-0983, www.bulguksa.or.kr)

Transport Info 🚗 From Gyeongbu Expressway 1, take Exit 9 (Gyeongju Interchange) and follow the signs into the city.

🚌 Buses depart for Gyeongju from Seoul, Busan, Gwangju, Daejeon, Daegu, Andong, and Gangneung.

🚆 The nearest train stations are Gyeongju Station (servicing regular trains—located downtown) and Singyeongju Station (KTX line—located on the outskirts of the city). Take bus No. 50, 60, 61, 70, 203, or 700 from the KTX station into Gyeongju.

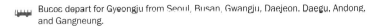

TIP

Where to Camp

Conveniently located 20 minutes southeast of Gyeongju city, and only minutes from Bulguk-sa, is the Toham-san Recreational Forest 토함산 자연휴양림. This city-operated campground is located in a mountainous area with lots of trees for shade. On the gravel-tiered hillside, you'll find several tent platforms installed for environmental ground protection. Within the campground complex are small and large cabins for rent, a swimming hole, and footpaths leading to a picnic area and a lookout point. This campground is easily accessible by car or taxi; unfortunately, bus access is limited.

🏠 San 599-1 Janghang-ri, Yangbuk-myeon, Gyeongju-si, Gyeongsangbuk-do
📞 054-772-1254
🕐 June to October
🎫 Entrance fee: 1,000 won (per person)
    Camping fee: 10,000 won (per tent)

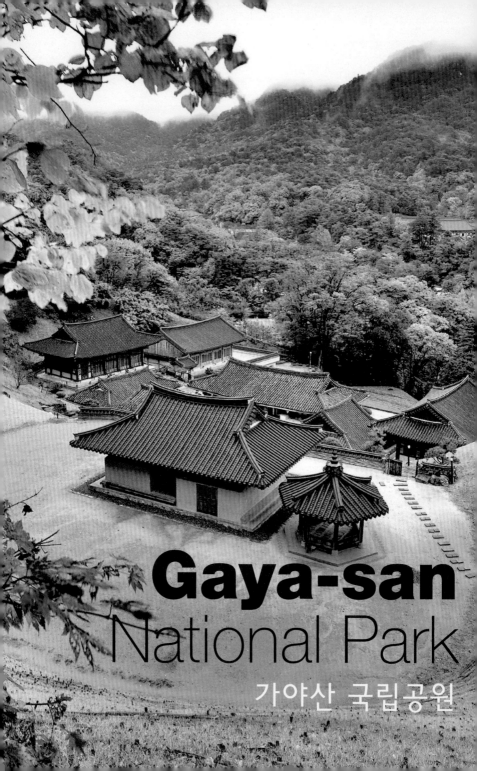

Gaya-san
National Park
가야산 국립공원

Highlights

1. Visit the famous temple of **Haein-sa** 해인사 and check out its historical cultural properties. Better yet, become a Templestay participant yourself.

2. Climb to one of the **hermitages**, such as **Hongje-am** 홍제암, **Wondang-am** 원당암, and **Baengnyeon-am** 백련암, near Haein-sa.

3. Feast on local cuisine at one of the many restaurants in the **tourist village of Chiin-ri** 치인리 .

4. Hike to the summit of **Sangwang-bong** 상왕봉—a pleasant early morning challenge.

Entrance of Haein-sa's Janggyeongpanjeon, the home of the *Tripitaka Koreana*

Known as the "mountain of wisdom and morality," Gaya-san is home to many historical and cultural spots. Revered as one of the three highest-ranking Buddhist temples in Korea, Haein-sa 해인사 is filled with ancient relics. This temple was added to UNESCO's World Heritage list in 1995. Korean Buddhists nationwide flock to this sacred place to enjoy the multitude of treasures tucked away within its walls, and to visit the many surrounding hermitages in the area. The temple houses four 15th century storage halls, referred to as the "Janggyeongpanjeon 장경판전." These structures protect the *Tripitaka Koreana* 고려대장경—a set of 81,258 wooden plates engraved with written sutras dating back to the 13th century. Named after the Haeinsammae in the *Avatamska Sutra*, this temple was built in the ninth century and now serves as a headquarters. Haein-sa also operates a Buddhist school and from out of this school many great monks have been trained.

Gaya-san's park boundaries lie within two provinces, Gyeongsangbuk-do and Gyeongsangnam-do. Haein-sa is easily accessible from 88 Olympic

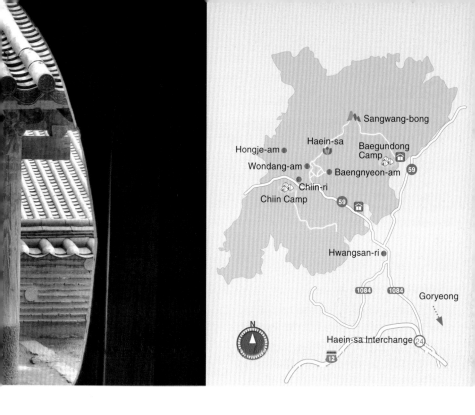

Expressway 12, as are the park's two campgrounds. Inside the park, local residents of the Chiin-ri 치인리 tourist village operate a wide array of restaurants and accommodations. These establishments are conveniently located across from the bus terminal. The first campground (in a group of three) is located 400 m uphill past the bus terminal and post office along the main road. Baegundong Campground 백운동 야영장 sits high on a mountainside, several kilometers away from Chiin-ri.

Like most mountain national parks, Gaya-san has extensive mountain trails. One trail in particular connects Baegundong Campground to Haein-sa by way of Sangwang-bong 상왕봉 (1,430 m). Another name for this peak is "Udu-bong 우두봉," so named because the shape resembles the head of a cow (*udu* in Korean). This track takes hikers through beautiful deciduous and coniferous forest.

🚩 Haein-sa (055-934-3110, www.haeinsa.or.kr)

Chiin
Campground
치인 야영장

⌂ San 20 Chiin-ri, Gaya-myeon,
　Hapcheon-gun, Gyeongsangnam-do
ⓒ 055-930-8000
⏰ July to August (Campground No. 2
　open all year round)

Campground No. 1

This campground is both an auto and forested camping site. Half the sites line up along the river fence, where campers have easy access to their vehicles and an older bathroom block. Although far from picture perfect, these sites attract families who erect large tents with lots of equipment. On the other side of the stream (accessible by footbridge) lies the forested campground. Most of the forested sites are on a downhill slant, which makes one ask, "What if it rains?" Those on the lower part of the hillside might expect mud runoff. These sites are also well worn by summer users, who seem to leave bits of picnic rubbish behind. A better time to camp at this location might be during spring or autumn, when there are fewer people.

Campground No. 2 (Yongmun)

Three hundred meters further uphill from Campground No. 1 is Chiin Campground No. 2. There is no parking lot, so campers will have to park their car at the lower campground and backpack their gear onto the site. This spot has only basic facilities, with water and a portable flush toilet trailer, but it is prettier, far less popular, cleaner, and well worth the walking effort. This location is the choice pick. The downside to this campground is the presence of bright night lamps that operate until early morning. Bring an eye mask if you want to sleep.

Campground No. 3 (Samjeong)

Another 100 m further uphill from Campground No. 2 is the third forested campground. This site has a newly constructed bathroom block with one shower stall and flush toilets. As with Campground No. 2, campers must backpack their gear onto the site, and night lamps are posted around the grounds. This, too, is a quiet pretty spot. Rental tents are set up at this location during peak season.

Transport Info From 88 Olympic Expressway 12, take Exit 24 (Haein-sa Interchange) and follow Regional Road 1084 onto Route 59. Follow the road signs to Haein-sa.

Buses depart from Daejeon (three times daily), Daegu (via Goryeong, 20 times daily), Jinju (three times daily), and Hamyang for the Chiin-ri tourist village and Haein-sa.

Ranger station at the entrance of Baegundong Campground

Baegundong
Campground
백운동 야영장

The view is superb at Baegundong, as this campground sits high on a steep mountainside. It has five grassy tiers with stone staircases leading from one to the next. Baegundong is located at the trailhead of Sangwang-bong, near the botanical garden and the elegant Gaya-san Tourist Hotel 가야산 관광호텔. The entire area is manicured, with a kind of refined beauty. Campers who don't like the cold shower at the campground can use the hotel sauna facilities for a small fee.

To get to the campground, campers will have to park their car in the large parking lot about 200 m away and backpack their gear onto the site. At this parking lot there is also a bus stop and ranger station. Because transportation to the campground is limited, another option might be to take a taxi from the village of Hwangsan-ri 황산리 (Gaya-myeon 가야면), which is serviced by numerous buses from Goryeong 고령.

🏠 1833-2 Baegun-ri, Suryun-myeon, Seongju-gun, Gyeongsangbuk-do
📞 054-932-3999
🕐 Open all year round

🔊 30+	🚻	👫 ✓	♿ ✓	🧎 ✓	🚲	🚿 ✓
🚬 ✓	🔥	🧺	🍴 ✓	⛲	ℹ️ ✓	

Transport Info From 88 Olympic Expressway 12, take Exit 24 (Haein-sa Interchange) and follow Regional Road 1084 to Route 59. You will come to a fork in the road where these two roads meet. Instead of going straight to Haein-sa, turn right and drive up the mountainside for about 5 km to Baegundong. Make a left turn there and drive 100 m farther to the parking lot and ranger station.

🚌 Buses depart from Goryeong (three times daily) and Seongju (two times daily).

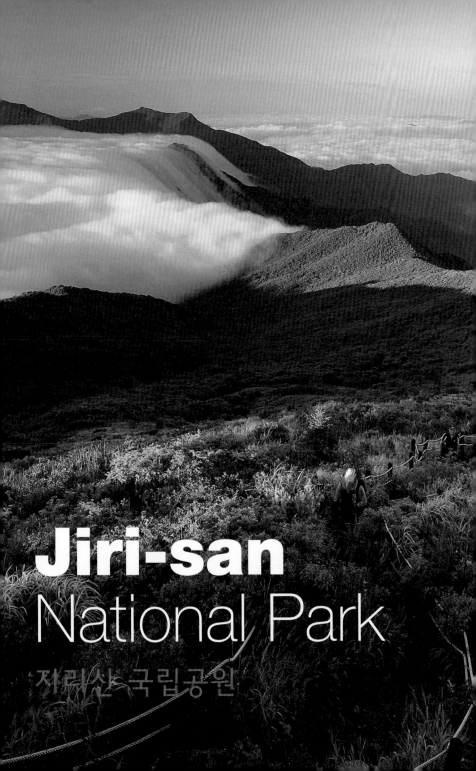

Jiri-san
National Park
지리산 국립공원

Highlights

1. Start at one end of the park and finish at the other while hiking along Jirisan's **extensive mountain ridge**. You will need to book a shelter for a night or two, depending on your destination.

2. Take **scenic Regional Road 861** or **1023** and enjoy the sights of tea plantations and mountain views.

3. Join a scheduled tour to see **Asiatic black bears** at the **Species Restoration Technology Institute** 종복원기술원.

4. Stroll through the three notable temples in Jirisan: **Hwaeom-sa** 화엄사, **Ssanggye-sa** 쌍계사, and **Daewon-sa** 대원사. Each has its own unique qualities, and each participates in the Templestay program.

Banya-bong, Jiri-san National Park

If mountains are the backbone to Korea's national parks, then Jiri-san, the largest of all mountain national parks, can be defined by its extensive mountain ridge trails, which only the experienced hiker dares attempt. Rising into the sky, Cheonwang-bong 천왕봉 stands as the second highest point in the country at 1,915 m, surpassed only by Halla-san 한라산 at 1,950 m. There is a multitude of trail possibilities for reaching this summit from various points in the park. Because of high mountain elevation, clouds that are too heavy with moisture cannot rise over the crest, and the moisture thus falls as rain. This, together with the hot summer temperatures, accounts for Jiri-san's lush bamboo bush undergrowth.

Only one major road runs through the park; all other access points are like tentacles that barely reach past the park boundaries. The majority of the park is not accessible by car and can only be crossed on foot. A series of mountain shelters situated along trails provides mountaineers with overnight accommodation.

Jirisan has two frontiers. One is to the north, where winters can be very cold. The other faces south into the sun, where tea plantations manage to thrive

in frosty winter temperatures. The southern frontier boasts of fruit orchards and beautiful leafy rows of tea plants lined uniformly across hillsides. In fact, scenic Regional Road 1023, not far from Ssanggye-sa 쌍계사, has the Hadong Tea Cultural Center 하동 차문화센터. This center houses both a green tea shop (for buying or just tasting) and a green tea museum. Buses from Hadong 하동 and Gurye 구례 travel along Regional Road 1023.

Since 2004, the park office has released 38 Asiatic black bears into the wild at Jiri-san, with the hope of increasing their numbers. Though exciting, the restoration project has faced unforeseen challenges such as protests by local residents, the setting of illegal bear traps, and the need to monitor bear movements to keep them out of harm's way. Four new cubs were born in 2012, bringing the total bear population up to 27. The Species Restoration Technology Institute 종복원기술원, beside Hwangjeon Auto Campground, operates an educational center with scheduled tours of a bear enclosure.

Wild boars and snakes also call Jiri-san National Park home. Caution and

Shelters Contact

1 Chibatmok Shelter 치밭목대피소

2 Jangteomok Shelter 장터목대피소

3 Rotary Shelter 로타리대피소 ── 055-972-7772

4 Yeonhacheon Shelter 연하천대피소

5 Byeoksoryeong Shelter 벽소령대피소

6 Seseok Shelter 세석대피소

7 Nogodan Shelter 노고단대피소 061-783-1507

8 Piagol Shelter 피아골대피소 061-783-1928

Viewing platform, Nogodan Peak

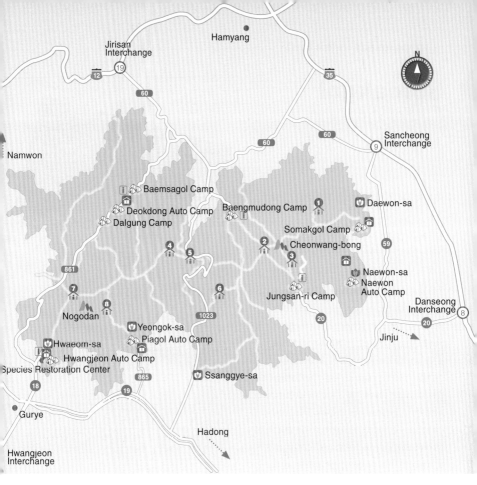

common sense are required should you cross paths with any of these creatures on a hiking trail. Visit a ranger station or visitor center for more information.

Not to be missed is the scenic drive along Regional Road 861. This road snakes its way up to the mountaintop (Nogodan 노고단), where you can find a viewing platform and trailheads. It then continues down the other side of the mountain toward other campgrounds. Buses from Namwon 남원 and Gurye travel up to Nogodan Mountain Pass along this road. Due to the elevation, this mountain pass is sometimes closed temporarily due to winter snowstorms.

Hwaeom-sa (061-782-7600, www.hwaeomsa.org)
Ssanggye-sa (055-883-1901, www.ssanggyesa.net)
Daewon-sa (055-974-1112, www.daewonsa.or.kr)

Somakgol Campground
소막골 야영장

San 118 Pyeongchon-ri, Samjang-myeon, Sancheong-gun, Gyeongsangnam-do
055-972-7775
April to November

This nice little forested campground is tucked away on a small parcel of land on the other side of the suspension bridge, across the river. The more private sites are at the back of the campground, on the top tier. The lower level has one field kitchen and one bathroom block. Should campers require information on trails or weather conditions, there is an information booth just beyond the restaurant, store, and bus stop.

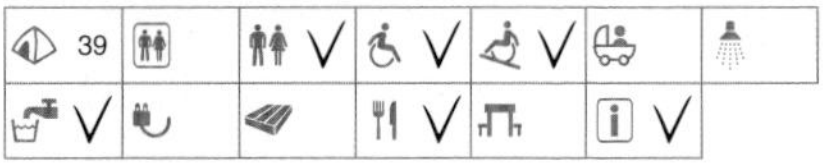

Transport Info

a) From Tongyeong-Daejeon Expressway 35 (mountain overpass route), take Exit 9 (Sancheong Interchange) and turn right onto Route 59 going south. Follow the brown and white signs to Daewon-sa 대원사.

b) From Tongyeong-Daejeon Expressway 35 (valley route), take Exit 8 (Danseong Interchange) and follow Route 20 onto Route 59 going north. Follow the signs to Jiri-san National Park and Daewon-sa.

Buses depart for Daewon-sa fifteen times daily from Jinju North Bus Terminal. Other buses depart for the temple from Busan (four times daily).

The nearest train station is Jinju Station.

Naewon
Auto Campground
내원 자동차야영장

For campers traveling by bus, Naewon Campground is a 20-minute walk from the bus stop. Walk toward the mountains along a narrow road that goes past a small row of pension houses. Keep to the left. There are road signs, but they are written in Korean. It might be a good idea to write out the Korean word for Naewon-sa 내원사 in case you need to ask someone for directions. The temple is located just past the campground along the same road.

Naewon Campground has both auto and forested sites. The more private forested section is at the back of the property, while the auto section is built in an open space at the front. During peak season, this area is popular with families, who swim in the nearby river.

⌂ 105-4 Naewon-ri, Samjang-myeon, Sancheong-gun, Gyeongsangnam-do
☎ 055-972-7775
☉ April to November

Transport Info From Tongyeong-Daejeon Expressway 35, take Exit 8 (Danseong Interchange) and follow Route 20 onto Route 59 going north. Follow the signs to Jiri-san National Park and Naewon-sa.

 Buses depart for Daewon-sa from Jinju North Bus Terminal (board the same bus as for Daewon-sa). Confirm your destination prior to boarding, and ask the driver to let you off at the nearest stop to Naewon-sa.

 The nearest train station is Jinju Station.

Jungsan-ri
Campground
중산리 야영장

⌂ 634-4 Jungsan-ri, Sicheon-myeon,
  Sancheong-gun, Gyeongsangnam-do
☏ 055-972-7785
⏱ Open all year round

⊲ 43	♦♦	♦♦ ✓	♿	♿	🚐	⚗
🗑 ✓	♨	⬗	🍴 ✓	🔀	ⅈ ✓	

Passengers traveling by bus are dropped off at the village of Jungsan-ri 중산리.
It is at least a 30-minute walk up the steep mountain road to the park entrance
and parking lot. Taxis frequently make the ten-minute shuttle run to and from
the gate for campers and hikers.

Located at the head of the shortest trail to the Cheonwang-bong, Jungsan-ri
Campground is 300 m farther from the parking lot, restaurants, park gate, and
visitor center. Campers must backpack their gear onto the site.

This lovely four-tiered forested campground cuts into the grassy hillside,
where tent sites are roped off one beside the other. There is one bathroom block
on site, as well as one field kitchen. The bathroom remains clean—as long as the
doors are kept closed at night to keep the bugs out!

Transport Info   From Tongyeong-Daejeon Expressway 35, take Exit 8 (Danseong Interchange) and
follow Route 20 to the end. Follow the signs to Jiri-san National Park and Jungsan-ri.

  Buses depart for Jungsan-ri from Jinju North Bus Terminal (sixteen times daily),
Busan (six times daily), and Masan.

  The nearest train station is Jinju Station.

Piagol
Auto Campground
피아골 자동차야영장

Located at the end of Piagol Valley 피아골계곡 at a distance of 2 km from the temple of Yeongok-sa 연곡사, this campground is reached by a road that rises slowly to a higher elevation where weather is cooler and damper and, in the winter, snowier. In the summer, families gather at the mountain stream across the road, where children wade in the cool and pristine water pools.

This campground has 40 square, grassy tent pads bordered by pavement, a layout that allows campers to park their car conveniently alongside their tent. What this ends up meaning is that one tent door opens onto another, with views of the surrounding vehicles rather than the beautiful mountain scenery. Pack food for this location. For those who want to hike to the ridge follow the trail past Yeongok-sa.

🏠 Naedong-ri, Toji-myeon, Gurye-gun, Jeollanam-do
📞 061-783-9110
🕐 July to August

| ⚓ 40 | 👫 ✓ | 👪 ✓ | ♿ ✓ | ♨ ✓ | 🚼 | 🚿 |
| 🚻 ✓ | 🔥 | 〰 | 🍴 ✓ | ⛩ | ℹ ✓ |

Transport Info   From Expressway 27, take Exit 3 (Hwangjeon Interchange) and follow the road signs to Gurye. Drive through the village of Guryegu along Route 17 and turn right over the village bridge onto Route 18. At the end of the bridge, turn left. Drive to and past the town of Gurye (eastside) along this route. At the northeast end of town, it will cross with Route 19. Take the underpass and follow the road signs to Hadong. Drive along Route 19 for about 12 km. Turn left onto Regional Road 865 and continue for about 9 km into the mountains. The campground is on the right side of the road just before the Yeongok-sa pay booth.

  Buses depart Gurye Bus Terminal for Piagol Valley (14 times daily). The campground is located 2 km before the temple of Yeongok-sa.

  The nearest train station is Guryegu Station, which is located 5 km south of the town of Gurye. Buses depart for Gurye from Guryegu (25 times daily).

Azalea blossoms along the Nogodan Trail, Jiri-san National Park

Hwangjeon
Auto Campground
황전 자동차야영장

Hwangjeon is a fully serviced campground located 1 kilometer south of the temple of Hwaeom-sa and 6 km north of Gurye. Gurye has a bus terminal, a couple of grocery stores, a swimming pool with a terrific view of the mountains, and a riverside bike path. Campers traveling by bus from Gurye, Gwangju, or Busan are dropped off at the tourist village bus stop near the park's visitor center. The campground is behind the visitor center on the other side of the river, next to the Species Restoration Technology Institute building.

Hwangjeon Auto Campground has both auto and forested camping sites. The forested area is made up of several tent pads cut into the hillside. These hidden spots are good for backpackers looking for privacy. The ground level has larger sites that are big enough for the tent and car. At the center of the campground is a newly built bathroom block. A hiking trail leads to Nogodan from Hwaeom-sa.

⌂ 41 Hwangjeon-ri, Masan-myeon, Gurye-gun, Jeollanam-do
ⓒ 061-780-7700
⊕ April to November

Transport Info   See Piagol Campground. When drivers get to the underpass, instead, follow the road signs to Hwaeom-sa. The campground is 6 km north of Gurye and 1 km south of Hwaeom-sa. (Note: Nearby is Regional Road 861, a scenic mountain overpass leading to the Dalgung, Deokdong, Baemsagol, and Baengmudong campgrounds on the other side of the mountain.)

  Buses depart for Hwaeom-sa from Gurye Bus Terminal (sixteen times daily) and Hadong Bus Terminal (ten times daily). Other buses depart from Gwangju and Busan.

  See Piagol Campground.

Dalgung
Campground
달궁 야영장

⌂ 274 Deokdong-ri, Sannae-myeon,
　 Namwon-si, Jeollabuk-do
☎ 063-625-8911
⊙ Open all year round

Auto Campground

Dalgung Auto Campground is a large and popular family camp. Built in an open space without a lot of trees or privacy, this campground is convenient for families who want to park their car alongside their tent. The tent pads have a grassy dirt foundation and most campsites are lit at night by street lamps. On site there is an older bathroom block, a few portable toilet trailers, a handful of field kitchens, a convenience store, and some electrical hookups.

Forested Campground

A half a kilometer down the road from the auto campground is a nice, small (although slightly rocky) pine-forested area. Maybe a little inconveniently for families with children, the only toilet block and parking lot are located on the other side of the road. When crossing the road, caution is required. One major feature of this campground is its close proximity to some great barbecue restaurants. Just follow your nose to the succulent smells of barbecued meat.

Transport Info From 88 Olympic Expressway 12, take Exit 19 (Jiri-san Interchange) and follow the signs for Jiri-san National Park into the village of Inwol 인월. Turn left at the road sign for Jiri-san. Go straight to the T-intersection and turn right onto Regional Road 60. Follow it onto Regional Road 861. The Baemsagol, Dalgung, and Deokdong campgrounds are located in close proximity to one another along this regional road. (Note: Regional Road 861 turns into a scenic mountain pass that leads to Hwangjeon Auto Campground on the other side of the mountain.)

🚌 Buses depart from Namwon Intercity Bus Terminal (ten times daily).

🚆 The nearest train station is Namwon Station.

Deokdong
Auto Campground
덕동 자동차야영장

This smaller seasonal campground is built in an open space sandwiched between the road and river. Popular during the summer months, this campground has a convenient layout for families who want to park their car alongside their tents. The prettier shaded sites rest along the riverside. There are five electric boxes here—when they're in full use, you will see a network of long extension cords leading to campsites in every direction. On the grounds, there are both portable and permanent bathroom blocks.

Transport Info   See Dalgung Campground.

⌂ 72 Deokdong-ri, Sannae-myeon, Namwon-si, Jeollabuk-do
ℂ 063-625-8911
🕐 April to November

Snow-covered peaks of Jiri-san loom behind the national park office

Baemsagol
Campground
뱀사골 야영장

⌂ 256 Buun-ri, Sannae-myeon, Namwon-
　si, Jeollabuk-do
☎ 063-625-8911
⏰ Open all year round

Auto Campground (No. 1)

This region is popular with families
who come to wade, on a hot summer's
day, in the pristine water pools of
the valley river, which stretches from
Baemsagol to Dalgung campgrounds.
The auto campground is in the shape
of a horseshoe with sandy gravel tent
pads on the outer side of the ring—
set in forest or along the riverside.
Restaurants across the road are
seasonal, so it is recommended to
pack food if camping outside of peak
summer.

⏏ 60	🚻 ✓	🚼 ✓	♿ ✓	🛋	🚐 ✓	🚿
🚰 ✓	⚓	◩	🍴 ✓	⛺ ✓	ℹ ✓	

Baemsagol Valley, Jiri-san

Forested Campground (No. 2)

Located past the gate and over the
bridge, this forested campground has
a hard dirt surface which gets rather
muddy when it rains. For this reason,
there are raised tent pads. Set among
lots of trees, rental tents are set up
at this location during peak season.
Because the parking lot is 200 m away,
campers will have to carry their gear
onto their site. Baemsagoal is at the
trailhead of the hiking route leading
to Samdo-bong 삼도봉 (1,499 m) and
Tokki-bong 토끼봉(1,534 m).

⏏ 30+	🚻 ✓	🚼 ✓	♿ ✓	🛋	🚐 ✓	🚿
🚰 ✓	⚓	◩	🍴 ✓	⛺	ℹ ✓	

Transport Info　　See Dalgung Campground.

Baengmudong
Campground
백무동 야영장

Almost like a garden maze, this very pretty campground is situated on a hillside with steep stone staircases leading up to various tiers with trees and plants growing as hedge fences. It is pleasant to the eye and located in the oddest of places—at the end of a small gravel road past an archway of *minbaks* and pension houses. The visitor center and bus stop are just 300 m from the campground. This location is superb for campers wanting to hike to Cheonwang-bong or other peaks in the vicinity, like Chotdae-bong 촛대봉 (1,703 m), Yeonha-bong 연하봉 (1,730 m), or Jeseok-bong 제석봉 (1,808 m).

◁ 75+	🕴 ✓	🚻 ✓	♿ ✓	⛲	🚿 ✓	⚲
🚰 ✓	🔥	🧺 ✓	🍴 ✓	🎋 ✓	ℹ ✓	

⌂ San 120, Gangcheong-ri, Macheon-myeon, Hamyang-gun, Gyeongsangnam-do
📞 055-963-1260
🕐 Open all year round

Transport Info From 88 Olympic Expressway 12, take Exit 19 (Jiri-san Interchange) and follow the signs for Jiri-san National Park into the village of Inwol. Turn left at the road sign for Jiri-san. Go straight to the T-intersection and turn right onto Regional Road 60. Follow this road onto Regional Road 1023. Where these two roads meet, you will see two bridges. Turn right and go over the second bridge (bypassing the village). Turn left at the end of the bridge. The road going to Baengmudong is the third on the left off of Regional Road 1023. Signage is clearly posted.

🚌 Buses depart for Baengmudong from Seoul (eight times daily), Daejeon (once daily), and Hamyang (seventeen times daily).

Hallyeo-
haesang
National Park

한려해상 국립공원

Highlights

1. Drive to the end of the Sangju · Geumsan district to enjoy the soft golden sands of **Sangju Silver Sand Beach** 상주 은모래비치. A locally run campground is in operation from mid-July to mid-August. This spot offers some really nice ocean swimming opportunities.

2. **Eat different types of fish** at local restaurants. From platters of thinly sliced raw fish to whole fried fish, raw oysters, and fish soups, there are lots of local dishes to try.

3. Tour a former **prisoner-of-war camp** 거제 포로수용소 that held 170,000 prisoners during the Korean War.

4. Take a ferry tour to the outer islands, many of which are uninhabited. **Somaemul-do** 소매물도 and the nearby **lighthouse island of Deungdaeseom** 등대섬 are sights to behold.

4

Windy Hill, Geoje-do

In the South Sea of Korea, hundreds of mountains rise out of the clear blue waters as coastal islands. With its ragged rock cliff formations and intimate beach coves, this scenery attracts millions of visitors yearly. Due to modern-day engineering, many large islands are now linked by bridge and are accessible by car or bus. Some travelers, however, prefer to take the 45- or 70-minute ferries that run from Masan 마산 and Busan 부산 to the island of Geoje-do 거제도.

Hallyeo-haesang is divided into six districts that cover a wide area between Yeosu 여수 in Jeollanam-do and Geoje-do in Gyeongsangnam-do. The districts (from west to east) are Odong-do 오동도 → Namhaedaegyo 남해대교 → Sangju 상주· Geum-san 금산 → Sacheon 사천 → Tongyeong 통영· Hansan 한산 → Geoje 거제· Haegeumgang 해금강. All districts provide daily use access; only one area, Geoje· Haegeumgang, operates a national park campground.

Tongyeong, a coastal city in the heart of Hallyeo-haesang National Park, benefits from a year-round mild oceanic climate. This is partly due to mountain barriers blocking South Sea winds. Historically linked to the figure of Admiral Yi Sun-Sin 이순신, the name Tongyeong means "command post." The legendary admiral was based on the nearby island of Hansan-do 한산도, and a full-scale

Dongpirang Mural Village, Tongyeong

model of his "turtle ship 거북선"—spiked with iron nails to discourage enemies from boarding—can be seen along Tongyeong's waterfront. Most tourist spots are found in and around Gangguan-hang 강구안항. You can find ferries to the pristine islands that dot the coastline, a traditional live fish market, the quirky murals of Dongpirang 동피랑, a sculpture park, and hiking to Nam-san 남산 Pavilion, which overlooks the port. At nearby Mireuk-san 미륵산, Korea's longest cable car is in operation. Measuring almost 2 km in length, it affords passengers spectacular views of Hallyeo-haesang National Park from a higher elevation.

Other popular tourist destinations located one hour by ferry from Tongyeong-hang 통영항 are Somaemul-do 소매물도 and the picturesque lighthouse island of Deungdaeseom 등대섬. With their landscapes of jagged, craggy cliffs and grassy meadows, the islands are connected by a small gravel causeway, which is 150 m long and can be accessed only two times a day during low tide.

The Geoje · Haegeumgang district has a number of sights to enjoy. A former POW Camp 거제 포로수용소 that held 170,000 prisoners during the Korean War is located in the town of Gohyeon 고현 in Geoje-do. Of those captured, twenty thousand were Chinese, and the rest North Koreans. This museum provides an opportunity for an education in war history that is unlike what you find at other war museums around the country.

Haegeumgang

Gujora Beach (top), Samcheonpo Bridge in Sacheon (bottom)

North of Hakdong Auto Campground 학동 사동차야영장 is Gujora Beach 구조라 해수욕장, a popular swimming place with golden sands. Ferry services run between the Oe-do 외도 botanical island park and the two docks of Hakdong and Gujora. South of the campground is the tiny, narrow peninsula of Haegeumgang 해금강, home to a hidden beach called Hammok 함목 해수욕장, a walking trail to Windy Hill 바람의 언덕, a ferry service, and scenic ragged cliffs. There is a circular scenic drive continuing farther south along Route 14 and onto Regional Road 1018, toward Myeongsa Beach 명사 해수욕장 and Mang-san 망산. The two-lane road is paved at first before turning into a single-lane gravel mountain road with multiple potholes. This back road route is not recommended for camping vans, trailers, or inexperienced drivers, but it has some lovely views from higher elevations.

TIP

Ferry Schedules

This national park has locally operated ferry services and tour boats to the many outer islands. In fact, if travelers plan well enough, it is quite possible to island-hop, although ferry and tour services are often canceled or delayed when the weather turns bad. This typically happens in monsoon season. In the winter, tour operators dramatically reduce their operation times, since there are so few visitors during this period.

Hakdong
Auto Campground
학동 자동차야영장

⌂ 221-1 Hakdong-ri, Dongbu-myeon,
　 Geoje-si, Gyeongsangnam-do
☎ 055-635-5421
🕐 Open all year round

| 🌊 170 | 🚻 | 🚶 ✓ | ♿ ✓ | 🛶 ✓ | 🚐 ✓ | 🚿 ✓ |
| 🚰 ✓ | 🔌 ✓ | 🛏 | 🍴 ✓ | 🪑 | ℹ ✓ |

This campground is across from Hakdong Pebble Beach 학동 흑진주 몽돌해변 on
the southeast coast of Geoje-do. Driving to and through this very popular
area during the summer season is slower than molasses, and the northern part
of coastal Route 14 is plagued with traffic lights. Patience and tolerance are
required. The good news—a newly constructed highway bypasses the small
town of Gohyeon, making the drive to Hakdong faster and easier.

　Situated among motels and restaurants, this campground makes camping
easy and caters to social gatherings. At night, families and youth gather by the
seaside to set off firecrackers, drink, and talk until the early morning hours.
Since visitors can pitch tents free of charge on the beach, the auto campground's
location across the road makes it a welcome refuge from beach activity.

　If you are looking for a way to spend your day, there is a rocky coastline not
far from the beach where many fishermen cast their line in the hopes of catching
their own seafood dinner. Bring a rod if you have one.

　Hakdong is divided into two sections, one that can accommodate up to
70 tents and another designed for up to 103 auto campsites—6 of which are

allotted to caravans. Special features at this park include an indoor kitchen, a sports ground, and a small stage for entertainment. At the time of this book's writing, Hakdong Auto Campground was closed for construction. The Korea National Park Service says that it will be open and fully operational by July 2013. Once built, the bathroom facilities will offer full services.

Transport Info 🚗 From Tongyeong-Daejeon Expressway 35, take Exit 1 (Tongyeong Interchange) and drive to the very end. Follow the signs along Route 14 going east toward Geoje. Drive for about 20 km to the city of Gohyeon (also spelled "Gohyun"). Just before entering the city, take the upper exit ramp for Okpo 옥포 and Jangseungpo 장승포 (Route 14). This newly constructed road bypasses Gohyeon. Drive for only a few kilometers before taking the first exit ramp to Regional Road 1018. At the bottom of the ramp, turn right and follow the signs for Hakdong Pebble Beach and Haegeumgang. The campground is about 15 km farther on along Regional Road 1018. Travelers who want to visit the POW camp should turn left at the bottom of the ramp and drive for about a kilometer. Signage is difficult to follow, so stay alert.

🚌 Buses No. 56 and 67 both depart ten times daily from Gohyeon Intercity Bus Terminal for Hakdong Pebble Beach. Travelers should expect reduced service in the winter. Buses depart for Gohyeon from Seoul, Daejeon, Jinju, and Busan.

🛥 Ferries depart from Busan and Masan for Gohyeon Passenger Ship Terminal. (Note: The Gohyeon Intercity Bus Terminal is across from the ferry dock.) Ferry passengers will need to transfer onto a public bus for Hakdong Pebble Beach. Other ferries depart from Busan for the Okpo and Jangseungpo Passenger Ship Terminals located on the east coast of the island, near Route 14.

SOUTHWEST

JEOLLABUK-DO | JEOLLANAM-DO | JEJU-DO

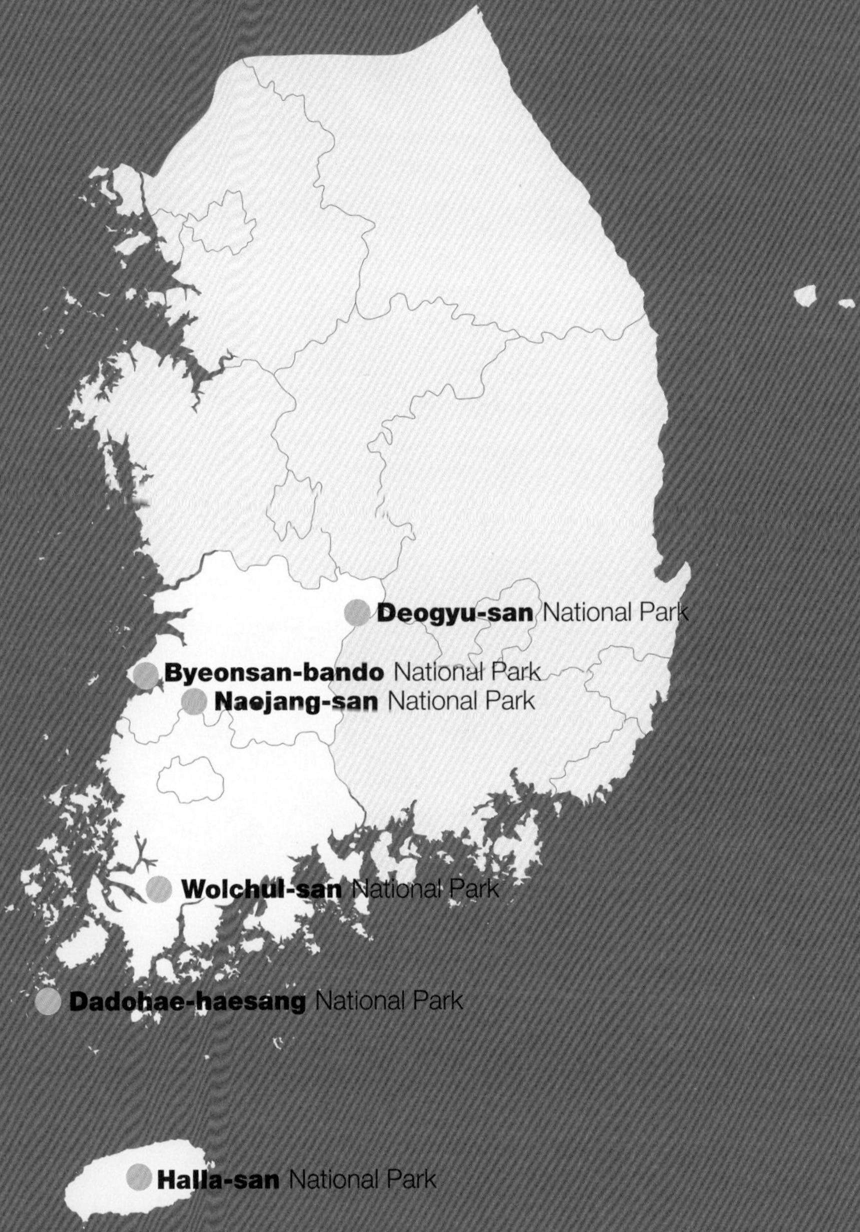

Deogyu-san National Park

Byeonsan-bando National Park
Naejang-san National Park

Wolchul-san National Park

Dadohae-haesang National Park

Halla-san National Park

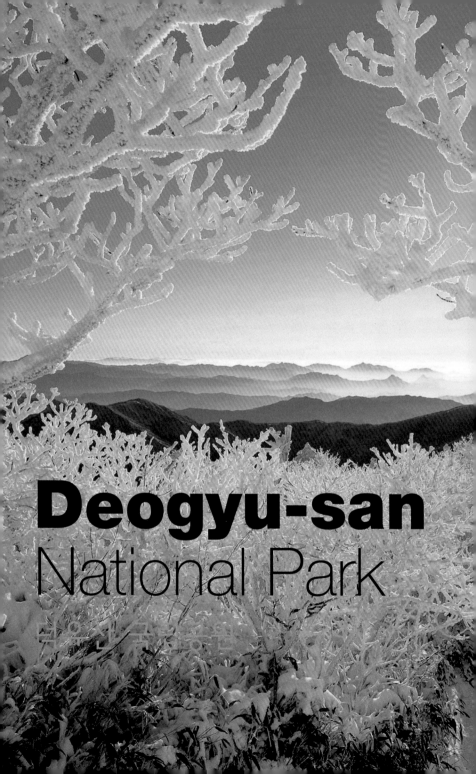

Deogyu-san
National Park

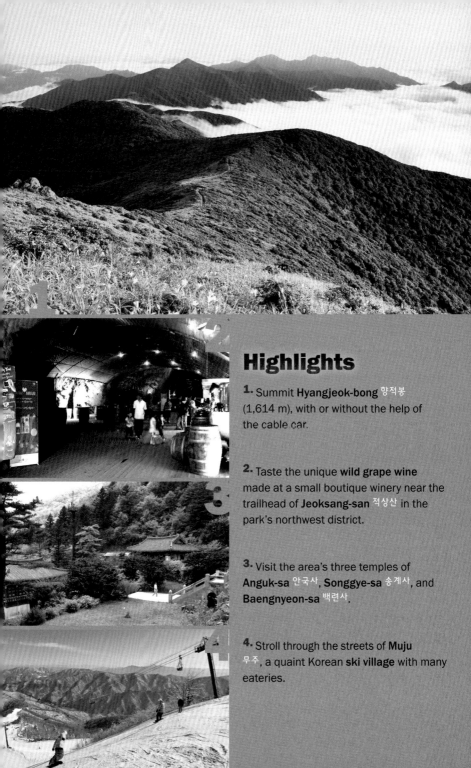

Highlights

1. Summit **Hyangjeok-bong** 향적봉 (1,614 m), with or without the help of the cable car.

2. Taste the unique **wild grape wine** made at a small boutique winery near the trailhead of **Jeoksang-san** 적상산 in the park's northwest district.

3. Visit the area's three temples of **Anguk-sa** 안국사, **Songgye-sa** 송계사, and **Baengnyeon-sa** 백련사.

4. Stroll through the streets of **Muju** 무주, a quaint Korean **ski village** with many eateries.

Muju Ski Resort, Deogyu-san National Park

High mountains and a ski resort are the two significant draws that bring hordes of visitors to this national park annually. Having the fourth highest peak at 1,614 m, Hyangjeok-bong 향적봉 can be conquered either on foot or with the help of a cable car from Muju Resort 무주리조트 (also known as Deogyusan Resort). The cable car operates all year round, with trails from the summit leading down to and past the campground in the Samgong 삼공 district. Mountaineers who wish to hike longer, more challenging trails have the option of sleeping overnight at one of the park's two shelters (see the map).

Deogyu-san is the only national park in the country that promotes wild grape wine. Winemaking using Western methods is a new business in Korea, although grapes have been cultivated for years where ideal growing conditions exist. In Deogyu-san National Park, grapevines can be found high up on the mountain slopes. Four small entrepreneurial wineries make wine with these grapes and one of them can be found on Jeoksang-san 적상산. The individual wineries welcome visitors and usually offer wine tasting for a small fee. For visitors on a limited schedule, there are two places with wine tasting bars that carry all local wine brands: the Wild Grape Wine Cave 머루와인동굴 (also called Meoru Wine Tunnel)

near Anguk-sa 안국사, and the Wine Gallery at Muju Resort.

Farther up the road from the Wild Grape Wine Cave is Anguk-sa. This temple sits at over 1,000 m above sea level. The views from it are stunning, and the switchback road to get there is an adventure in itself. While driving the switchbacks, watch out for the fearless chipmunks crossing the road. The temple hosts a small museum, a teahouse, and a short trail to Jeoksang-san Fortress 적상산성. About a kilometer past the Anguk-sa turnoff is the observation tower, which looks like a huge water tank with a spiral staircase. From the top, you can get a bird's eye view of this beautiful mountainous park.

In the mon th of June, the region hosts the annual Muju Firefly Festival 무주 반딧불축제. As human development creeps into natural territory, there has been an outpouring of genuine concern for the survival of the firefly species. As a result, the insect has been designated Natural Monument No. 322, and a festival featuring public awareness activities has been named in its honor. The insect theme park of Bandi Land 반디랜드 is home to an insect museum that includes a recovery center for the firefly, a botanical garden, and an astronomical observatory. Deogyu-san National Park hosts a number of activities for people of all ages.

Deogyudae
Campground
덕유대 야영장

⌂ San 60-5 Samgong-ri, Seolcheon-
   myeon, Muju-gun, Jeollabuk-do
℗ 063-322-3173
🕒 April to October (Auto campground
   open all year round)

This park operates the single largest national park campground in the country, with over 320 campsites. The national park office claims that there are 400 sites available (for 10,000 people), but families often occupy two sites—one for sleeping and the other for eating. Deogyudae Campground has both auto and forested sites.

A moonlight view in Deogyu-san

Auto Campground

This small, compact auto campground located 300 m from the park gate hosts a number of facilities ranging from showers and flush toilets to electricity and an on-site store that sells wood for campfires. This is a typical-looking auto campground where tents are erected side-by-side and among vehicles.

| 🔦 70 | 🚻 | ♂♀ ✓ | ♿ ✓ | 🛋 ✓ | 🛒 | 🚿 ✓ |
| 🚰 ✓ | 🧺 ✓ | 🛏 | 🍴 ✓ | 🪑 | ℹ️ ✓ |

Forested Campgrounds (Campground No. 1–6)

Three hundred meters past the auto campground is a very large forested hillside with hundreds and hundreds of tent pads. To get there, take the footpath located across from the auto campground, or follow the road.

This very large area is divided into six sections. The more popular sites at the base of the hill are car accessible and can accommodate large tents. As you work your way up the steep hill, the tents become sparser, probably because it requires more climbing effort. There are a few electric boxes, but tents camouflage the units, making it a game of hide and seek—especially during the busy season. Campers often bring their own long extension cords to plug into the bathroom blocks.

This campground has tents (peak season only), caravans, and cabins for rent. Just beyond the campground is an amphitheater, which is used for special events. The staff members at the park office are very helpful should you need maps or park information. Another, smaller information booth is located near a trailhead 200 m past the auto campground.

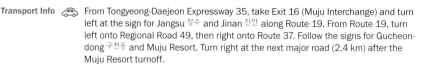

Transport Info 🚗 From Tongyeong-Daejeon Expressway 35, take Exit 16 (Muju Interchange) and turn left at the sign for Jangsu 장수 and Jinan 진안 along Route 19. From Route 19, turn left onto Regional Road 49, then right onto Route 37. Follow the signs for Gucheon-dong 구천동 and Muju Resort. Turn right at the next major road (2.4 km) after the Muju Resort turnoff.

🚌 Buses depart from Muju (ten times daily), Seoul (once daily), Gwangju (seven times daily), Daejeon (four times daily), and Jeonju (three times daily) for the Gucheon-dong bus stop in the Samgong district. Gucheon-dong is located 500 m from the auto campground. From Muju, a free shuttle bus goes to and from Muju Resort six times daily (with more frequent service in the winter).

Byeonsan-bando
National Park

변산반도 국립공원

Highlights

1. Walk along the peaceful 600-meter fir forest leading to the seventh century temple of **Naeso-sa** 내소사.

2. Take the ferry to **Wi-do** 위도, with its small island communities and beach.

3. Explore **fishing markets** and **fishing villages** along the coastal ring.

4. Enjoy an early morning mountain hike and an afternoon swim in the ocean, or slither your way through the mud flats with oozing mud between your toes.

5. Drive across the longest seawall in the world (over 33 km). **Saemangeum Seawall** 새만금 방조제 connects the cities of Gunsan 군산 and Buan 부안. Once completed, it will create future farming opportunities.

Like a rippling pond of rings, Byeonsan-bando National Park has as its core a small mountain range, with Uisang-bong 의상봉 the highest peak at 508 m. This mountain range offers visitors pleasant day-hiking opportunities. Wrapped around the mountain range is an agricultural strip made up of rice paddies and fruit and vegetable farms. Strawberries are among the fruits cultivated in this region. When it's in season, travelers are enticed by freshly picked produce at roadside stands. The final and outermost ring of the park is made up of fishing villages, tidal flats, and beaches.

One shoreline in particular stands out from the rest. Along a small, scenic coastal road between Gyeok-po 격포 and Gosa-po 고사포, visitors during low tide can seek out narrow trails leading to a rocky shoreline with stratified cliffs, hidden beaches, and tidal flats. And where there are tidal flats, there are families gathered with pails and picks to do their own clam digging. You can do the same if so inclined. This shoreline is also home to two popular tourist sites, the Chaeseokgang 채석강 and Jeokbyeokgang 적벽강 cliffs, which are about a kilometer apart from each other. This is an easy hike: start from the village of Gyeok-po and follow the coastal road southwest of the village to Chaeseokgang. Then retrace

Chaeseokgang Cliffs

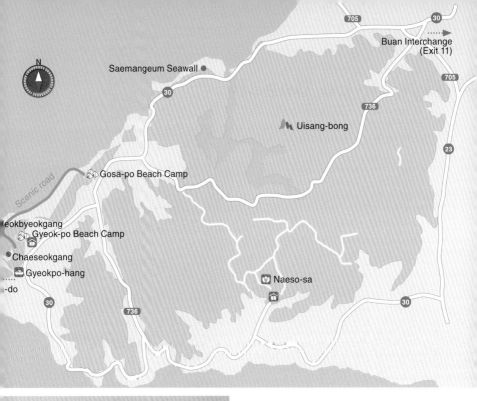

your track and hug the coastal road going northwest of the village to get to Jeokbycokgang. People gather at these two cliffs to witness the setting sun.

The two campgrounds operated by Korea National Park Service are located at the northwest tip of the finger peninsula along Route 30. These campgrounds are about 6 km apart from each other and can be easily reached by public transit from the small city of Buan 부안. The ranger station, located at the entrance of Naeso-sa 내소사, carries maps and trail information.

Naeso-sa (063-583-7281, www.naesosa.org)

Gyeok-po Beach
Campground
격포 야영장

⌂ Gyeokpo-ri, Byeonsan-myeon, Buan-gun,
  Jeollabuk-do
℅ 063-583-2054
⊙ Open all year round

🔊 30+	🚻	👫 ∨	♿	🏄	🚐 ∨	🚿
🚰 ∨	🔥	🛏	🍴 ∨	⛲ ∨	ℹ ∨	

Located 100 m from the beach, this campground is situated just on the outskirts of town 500 m from the bus terminal. Travelers coming from the terminal should walk over the small wooden bridge and follow the road signs to Gyeok-po Beach 격포 해수욕장.

   The campground is a small square parcel of land with a grassy gravel foundation. Because the bathroom facilities along the boardwalk are shared with the general public, it's a challenge to maintain a clean washroom. This second-rate beach is situated among motels, restaurants, stores, and amusement rides; campers should anticipate a party-like atmosphere. All is not lost, though— there is a ferry dock (Gyeokpo-hang 격포항) in town that takes passengers to and from the island of Wi-do 위도, located 14 km from the mainland.

Transport Info From Seohaean Expressway 15, take Exit 11 (Buan Interchange) and drive along Route 30 going west past Buan. Follow the road signs to Gyeok-po.

 Bus No. 100 departs from Buan for the town of Gyeok-po and goes to both campgrounds, Gyeok-po and Gosa-po. The bus stop is across from the express bus terminal just past the intersection. Other buses depart for the town of Gyeok-po from Gwangju, Jeonju, Jeongeup, and Iksan.

Gosa-po Beach
Campground
고사포 야영장

Stretching for just short of a kilometer and measuring 100 m in width, this pretty pine-forested campground can accommodate over 100 tents. In summer, it's a popular family vacation spot—which would explain the tidbits of garbage embedded in the pine needle flooring left behind from previous users.

While this campground parallels the beach and sits just behind it, a paved road runs the length of the campground, permitting campers to park their car alongside their tent. At the center of the campground stands a small military installation.

⌂ 441-11 Unsan-ri, Byeonsan-myeon, Buan-
   gun, Jeollabuk-do
✆ 063-583-2054
⊕ Open all year round

⊲ 100+	🚻		🚶 ∨	♿ ∨	🛶 ∨	🚐 ∨	🚿 ∨
🚰 ∨	⚲	🛏		🍴 ∨	🎪	ℹ

Transport Info   See Gyeok-po Campground. If you take a bus, tell the driver that you want to get off at Gosa-po Campground, or else the driver may not stop.

Naejang-san
National Park
내장산 국립공원

Highlights

1. Visit the park at the height of **autumn foliage**, when fall colors paint the forests with deep, rich colors of gold, orange, and red.

2. Ride up the **mountain cable car** to enjoy the views from the top, and follow a short trail to a viewing platform.

3. Experience the Templestay program at **Baegyang-sa** 백양사. The program at this temple is also offered in English.

4 Hike the peaks from **Bulchul bong** 불출봉 to **Yeonja-bong** 연자봉. This horseshoe-shaped trail is a full day's course. Keep in mind that there is always the option of ascending or descending by cable car.

Manicured gardens with tree-lined roads, hillside parks, walking and biking trails, hiking courses, a mountainside cable car, and two notable temples—these are the defining features of Naejang-san National Park. In other words, there is a lot to see and do in and outside the park. A lovely bike trail just on the other side of Naejang Reservoir 내장 저수지 heads into the village of Jeongeup 정읍, where groceries and local restaurants are readily available. If you prefer, drive the back road from the Naejang-sa 내장사 tourist village to Baegyang-sa 백양사 via Regional Road 49. Along this route are scenic mountain views, rice paddies, and fruit orchards.

The mountain forests of Naejang-san are made up of many maple trees. The park is especially beautiful during late October. Hidden in these forested mountains are two valley roads, wherein lie the two campgrounds. One campground is at the north end of the park, and the other in the south. Both have easy access to mountain trails. At the north end is a popular hiking trail to peaks in the formation of an amphitheater.

At the end of October, Jeongeup hosts an annual fall festival, with typical activities including face painting, rope skipping, arm wrestling competitions, entertainment, and food booths. But the festival's real drawing card is the bullfighting. Like sumo wrestlers, two bulls are brought into a small sandy ring, where they lock horns and go head to head with brute force until one pushes the other into defeat. Points are awarded for various successes, but fear not, the animals are not harmed. The festival location is at the end of the reservoir, about 2 km from Naejang Campground.

Baegyang-sa
(061-392-0434, www.baekyangsa.org)
Naejang-sa
(063-538-8741, www.naejangsa.org)

Naejang
Campground
내장 야영장

⌂ 92-2 Naejang-dong, Jeongeup-si,
  Jeollabuk-do
☎ 063-538-7875~7
🕐 Open all year round

The Naejang-san tourist village bus terminal is located 1.2 km past the campground. Five hundred meters beyond the terminal is the park gate leading to the temple of Naejang-sa, along with a visitor center and a cable car.

Naejang Campground might be a little difficult to find, since there is no clear signage or bus stop nearby. The campground is situated at parking lot No. 3, and it is accessible from both sides of the loop road. The nicer campsites are tucked away at the back of the property, set among trees and along a small river. This campground has clean bathroom facilities and a shower trailer.

Transport Info From Honam Expressway 25

> a) Take Exit 20 (Jeongeup Interchange) and follow Route 29 onto Regional Road 49. Park signs are clearly posted along these routes.
>
> b) Take Exit 19 (Naejang-san Interchange) and follow the road signs to Naejang-san Mountain. This route enters the north end of the park by the Naejang Reservoir, bypassing the town of Jeongeup.

> Buses depart for the tourist village from Jeongeup (No. 155 and No. 171—the bus stop is outside the bus terminal near the taxi stand) and Gwangju (five times daily). Other buses depart for Jeongeup from Seoul, Gwangju, Jeonju, Buan, Mokpo, Daegu, Daejeon, and Busan.

> The nearest train station is Jeongeup Station, which services regular and KTX trains. The station is located 200 m from the bus stop.

Gain
Campground
가인 야영장

Located beside the river about 400 m past the gate entrance, Gain Campground is within easy walking distance to Baegyang-sa and the information booth. On the grassy grounds there are a few picnic tables, a water station, a portable trailer with flush toilets, and electric boxes intalled throughout the camp. Just at the entrance of the campground is a newly constructed bathroom block built for campers and the general public.

⌂ 108 Yaksu-ri, Bukha-myeon, Jangseong-gun, Jeollanam-do
✆ 061-392-7288
🕑 April to November

◁》 50+	👫		👫 ✓	♿ ✓	⛵ ✓	🚲 ✓	🚿
⛽ ✓	🚰 ✓	🛏	🍴 ✓	⛩ ✓	ⓘ ✓		

Transport Info From Honam Expressway 25, take Exit 18 (Baegyang-sa Interchange) and follow the National Park and Baegyang-sa signs along Route 1. Signage is clearly posted.

 Buses depart for Baegyang-sa from Baegyang-sa Bus Terminal (21 times daily) and Gwangju (eleven times daily). Other buses depart for Baegyang-sa Bus Terminal from Gwangju, Jangseong, Jeongeup, Sokcho, Pyeongtaek, Songtan, and Osan.

 The nearest train station is Baegyang-sa Station, which is located 150 m from Baegyang-sa Bus Terminal.

Wolchul-san
National Park

월출산 국립공원

Highlights

1. Climb up to and cross the amazing **Cloud Bridge** 구름다리, which is constructed high up within the mountain range.

2. Be mesmerized by the **rolling hills of a green tea plantation**. Near Gyeongpodae Campground 경포대 야영장 is a viewing platform, which provides a calming setting, especially under a black starlit sky.

3. Take a day drive around the park visiting the local sights of temples (**Dogap-sa** 도갑사 and **Muwi-sa** 무위사) and **the historical village of Gurim** 구림마을. Notable scholars from this region have left their mark on Korean history.

What makes Wolchul-san different from other national parks, other than it being the smallest in Korea? Set in the heart of authentic Korean countryside, and the absence of loud tourist features in the surrounding area, make this park special. Other distinctive traits include its jagged pinnacle peaks, a suspension bridge, a rolling hillside green tea plantation, and two historic cultural properties (the temples of Dogap-sa 도갑사 and Muwi-sa 무위사), all of which contribute to its unique peaceful beauty. Wolchul-san is nature at its best, without a lot of public imposition.

The climbing courses to the highest peak, Cheonhwang-bong 천황봉 (809 m), lead hikers through bamboo bush, along waterfalls, and up ladders and rungs. The route via Saja-bong 사자봉 is humbling, as climbers make their way around rock pinnacles going to or coming from the incredible Cloud Bridge 구름다리, which connects two rocks and stands 120 m high, 60 cm wide, and 52 m long.

Pampas grass field, Wolchul-san

Wolchul-san has three major access points, two of which have campgrounds. Both are accessible from Route 13, which follows the perimeter of half the national park. Inconveniently to say the least, bus services for Cheonhwang Campground 천황 야영장 only operate out of the town of Yeongam 영암, and for Gyeongpodae Campground 경포대 야영장 out of the town of Seongjeon 성전.

Dogap-sa (061-473-5122, http://dogapsa.org)

Cloud Bridge

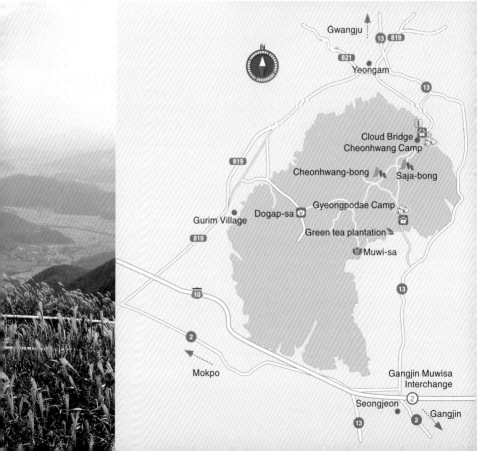

Cheonhwang
Campground
천황 야영장

🏠 98-9 Gaesin-ri, Yeongam-eup, Yeongam-
  gun, Jeollanam-do
📞 061-471-7614
🕐 Open all year round

| 🔊 25+ | 🚻 | 🚹🚺 ✓ | ♿ | ♿ | 👶 | 🚿 ✓ |
| 🚰 ✓ | 🔥 | 🧼 ✓ | 🍴 ✓ | 🏓 | ℹ️ ✓ |

Cheonhwang Campground is located 300 m from the park gate. It is situated in a forest on a hillside where there are over 25 wooden platforms upon which to pitch tents. The site includes two bathroom blocks, two field kitchens, and a shower room. If you plan to climb to Cheonhwang-bong or the Cloud Bridge, this campground is ideally located for an early morning start. Near the campground are a number of other amusements: a sculpture park, a nature trail, and a visitor center with a small museum. Restaurants and parking lots are located by the park gate entrance. Since parking space at the campground is limited, campers might be asked to park by the gate and walk up.

Transport Info **Access from the North**
Take Route 13 going south of Gwangju 광주 and Naju 나주. Continue to follow this route through and to the east of Yeongam. Exit at the last road sign for Wolchul-san National Park and Cheonhwang-sa 천황사. The campground is ten minutes from the village.

Access from the South
From Expressway 10, take Exit 2 (Gangjin Muwisa interchange) and follow signs to Route 13 going north to Yeongam. The Cheonhwang-sa and Gyeongpodae campgrounds are 14 km and 5 km north of Seongjeon, respectively. (Note: This newly constructed highway bypasses the south end of Wolchul-san and stretches from Yeongam to Suncheon with six new interchanges. Exit 2 lies just north of Seongjeon.)

🚌 Buses depart from Yeongam Bus Terminal five times daily for the Cheonhwang Campground park gate. If you don't want to wait for the bus, it is a ten-minute taxi ride from the terminal to the park gate entrance. Buses depart for Yeongam from Seoul, Mokpo, Gwangju, Incheon, Seongnam, and Bucheon.

On the other side of Cheonhwang-bong alongside a pristine mountain stream is Gyeongpodae Campground. This isolated and tranquil forested site is located 450 m from the park gate and parking lot. Campers must backpack their gear onto the site. This is nature at its best, with no car access or excessive public noise. Less popular than Cheonhwang Campground, this spot is a hidden gem. Pack a flashlight and food for this location.

If you are looking for ways to spend your day, the temple of Muwi-sa is located only 2.5 km from the park gate. A tea house is in operation at its entrance. This temple lies on the far side of a picturesque green tea plantation. For another alternative, consider spending a hot summer's afternoon soaking in the cool spring water pools of the park's stream.

Gyeongpodae
Campground
경포대 야영장

⌂ San 116-6 Wolnam-ri, Seongjeon-myeon, Gangjin-gun, Jeollanam-do
📞 061-432-7921
🕐 July to August

| ◁⏻ 20+ | ⍾ | ⍾ ✓ | ♿ | ⛷ | 🚌 | ☂ |
| 🚰 ✓ | ♨ | ⬗ | 🍴 ✓ | ⛲ | ℹ ✓ | |

Transport Info

🚗 See Cheonhwang Campground. Gyeongpodae Campground is 9 km farther along Route 13.

🚌 Buses depart from Seongjeon Bus Terminal six times daily for Gyeongpodae Campground park gate. Buses depart for Seongjeon from Gwangju, Mokpo, and Busan.

Dadohae-
haesang
National Park
다도해 해상 국립공원

Highlights

1. **Go island hopping** and explore isolated places and small village islands in the West and South Seas.

2. **Bask in the hot summer sun** at one of the many beaches in the region.

3. Bike the larger islands like **Jo-do** 조도, **Docho-do** 도초도, and **Bigeum-do** 비금도. These islands are bike-friendly and offer quality paved roads.

4. Check out the "**Miracle of Moses**" in **Jindo**—officially known as the Landing Tide Phenomenon. In March, a 2.8 kilometer-long, 40-meter wide tidal spit makes crossing on foot possible.

5. Unique to Korea is the indigenous dog of the Jindo area, appropriately called the **Jindo dog** 진돗개. The Jindo Dog Center can be found on the outskirts of the town of Jindo.

6. Climb up to the beautiful **Hyangil-am** 향일암 hermitage.

For travelers who have time to explore the southwestern outer islands, Dadohae-haesang National Park will not dissapoint them. The scenery is stunning and the islands are unique. The name Dadohae-haesang literally means "archipelago marine." The park covers several coastal districts encompassing 1,760 islands, 269 of which are uninhabited. And it is situated between the cities of Mokpo 목포 and Yeosu 여수.

The districts are (from west to east) Heuksan-do 흑산도 · Hong-do 홍도 → Bigeum-do 비금도 · Docho-do 도초도 → Jo-do 조도 → Soan-do 소안도 · Cheongsan-do 청산도 → Geomun-do 거문도 · Baek-do 백도 → Naro-do 나로도 → Geumo-do 금오도.

Dadohae-haesang islands are made up of a combination of forested mountains, flat coastal roads, and shorelines of white sand, pebbles, and rock. The islands'

seclusion (some more so than others) makes for bike-friendly exploration, as well as enjoyable hikes to small summits with scenic views at higher elevations, and some terrific swimming in small to large beach coves. The beach waters vary from clear to murky depending on the ocean currents, season, and seabed type.

Because the islands are difficult to reach, many of them are untouched by the tourism industry. Furthermore, young people raised in these secluded spots tend to move to the mainland in search of a different future, leaving the older generation behind. Visitors traveling to this part of the country will experience Korea in a different way. Authentic village life is community based and laid-back, and villagers are not only curious about foreigners, but also helpful. Some places almost take you back to another time. You can find street markets, narrow

alleyways, dry stone walls encasing fields, old toilet blocks designed only for small-framed people, hipped Asian roofs, women balancing baskets on their heads, weathered face lines, good humor, and an unspoken gentleness. Make no mistake: outside of large cities, Korean rural life has not lost itself completely in Western ways.

Yeosu has just this kind of combination of the plain charms of a Korean country village and gorgeous natural scenery. The host city for the

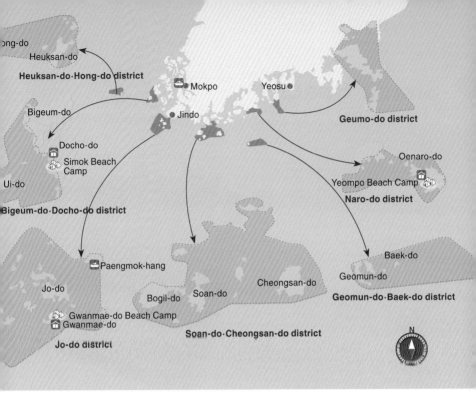

2012 World Expo, it is located midway between the east and west coasts on a small finger peninsula facing the South Sea. Its cool summers, mild winters, and long springs and autumns make it an ideal tourist stop. Popular tourist features in the area include ferry service to countless islands, the wetlands of Suncheon Bay 순천만, and the must-see Buddhist hermitage of Hyangil-am 향일암, with its narrow trail leading visitors through a cavern onto a spectacular cliffside temple with stunning views. On the outer islands, the beautiful red spring camellia blossoms of Odong-do 오동도 (part of Hallyeo-haesang National Park) and the 1905 lighthouse of Geomun-do 거문도 draw Korean travelers from all over the country.

   Dadohae-haesang has three National Park campgrounds, all of them on islands: Simok Beach Campground 시목 야영장 on Docho-do in the Bigeum-do · Docho-do district, Gwanmae-do Beach Campground 관매도 야영장 on Gwanmae-do in the Jo-do district, and Yeom-po Beach Campground 염포 야영장 on Oenaro-do in the Naro-do district. The first two are accessible only by ferry, while the last can be reached by car or bus.

1. Geomun-do Lighthouse
2. Fishing village, Gwanmae-do
3. Stone walls and canola flowers, Cheongsan-do

Simok Beach
Campground
시목 야영장

⌂ 965-2 Oryu-ri, Docho-myeon, Sinan-
gun, Jeollanam-do
✆ 061-284-9115
⏱ Open all year round

⚓ 75+	🚻	🚹🚺 ✓	♿ ✓	🛶	🚐	🚿 ✓
🚰 ✓	⚓	🏄 ✓	🍴 ✓	⛽ ✓	ℹ️	

Simok Beach Campground is located about 6 km from the ferry dock and is serviced by the only island road, Route 2. Docho-do and its sister island Bigeum-do (connected by bridge) are free of car hassles, making them great for bicycle exploration. These islands have secondary paved roads that lead to farming and fishing communities. Visitors traveling by bike have the added advantage of being independent, since transportation on the island is limited.

At this campground, visitors have the option of pitching their tent on the white sandy beach, in the forest, or on wooden platforms. There are two bathroom blocks, one at either end of the campground. Both have showers that inevitably get gritty from users tracking in sand. Near the campground area are a couple of restaurants and *minbaks*. Campers should pack food for this location, as the nearest village store is 2 km away. Another 2 km farther is an even bigger town with a larger grocery store. The ranger station is 2.7 km from the campground.

How to Get to Mokpo Coastal Ferry Terminal

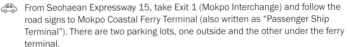

From Seohaean Expressway 15, take Exit 1 (Mokpo Interchange) and follow the road signs to Mokpo Coastal Ferry Terminal (also written as "Passenger Ship Terminal"). There are two parking lots, one outside and the other under the ferry terminal.

Express buses are available from most major cities. Once in Mokpo, travelers will need to flag a taxi or take a public bus (No. 1, 1-1, or 1-2) to Mokpo Coastal Ferry Terminal.

Mokpo is served by regular trains and the KTX line from Seoul. Once in Mokpo, travelers will need to get a taxi or take a public bus to Mokpo Coastal Ferry Terminal.

How to Get to Docho-do from Mokpo

Ferries depart Mokpo Coastal Ferry Terminal for Docho-do multiple times daily. In the terminal, the express boat and car ferry ticket counters can be found on either side of the escalator. Different companies operate different ferry services at different rates (see p. 33 for ferry contact numbers). The following is an example of the most frequent service, the slowest boat and the least expensive. Departures are at 7, 11:30 am, 1, and 3 pm at a cost of 10,200 won, and the journey is two and a half hours long. By express boat, the trip takes one hour and costs more. Departure times and rates may change at the discretion of the operator.

How to Get to Simok Campground from the Docho-do Ferry Dock

Bus transportation on the island is limited. Twice daily, passengers are picked up from the ferry terminal (9:40 am and 3:40 pm) and dropped off at the entrance of Simok en route, and twice daily passengers are picked from the Simok entrance (7:30 am and 1:30 pm) and dropped off at the ferry terminal. Campers should be aware that the bus service is laid-back. At the time of this book's writing, the bus was under repair, and there was no campground transport service. When a town employee was asked to provide a bus schedule and bus route, the employee said, in jest, that "only the bus driver knows." A faster, more reliable method of transportation is via bicycle or taxi.

Taxis charge about 8,000 won for the trip from the ferry terminal to the campground. However, finding a taxi for the return trip might be a challenge.

Gwanmae-do Beach
Campground
관매도 야영장

⌂ San 106-2 Gwanmae-ri, Jodo-myeon,
   Jindo-gun, Jeollanam-do
℡ 061-544-0151
⊙ Open all year round

Gwanmae-do has a beautiful beach that is long, wide, sandy, and clean. Because this entire island is a national park, great efforts have gone into keeping it naturally preserved. The narrow lanes, old stone walls, and huge magnolia tree (designated as Natural Monument Treasure No. 212) still remain. Even the forest here is greener, the sky bluer, the sunsets prettier, and the black starlit nights more impressive.

Gwanmae-do Beach Campground is a 300-meter walk from the ferry dock. With land capacity for only 40 tents, this small but beautiful forested campground has two well-maintained bathroom blocks, three water stations, and a public shower building near the beach.

The island is home to three small village communities. The village closest to the campground has a few restaurants, *minbaks*, and convenience stores that sell snack foods. Because restaurants depend on ferry services to deliver food supplies, the menu choice on the island is limited. Pack food for this location. Park ranger services are available on this campground. The staff at the ranger station can provide information on the island's mountain trails.

How to Get to Paengmok-hang 팽목항 on Jin-do 진도

 From Route 2 (about 38 km east of Mokpo and 9 km northwest of Gangjin 강진), take Route 13 going south to Haenam 해남. At the town of Haenam, Route 13 merges into Route 18. Follow Route 18 to and past the town of Jindo going to Paengmok-hang. Road signs to Haenam, Jindo, and Paengmok are clearly posted.

 Buses depart from Jindo Bus Terminal five times daily for Paengmok-hang (located an hour away). Bus arrival and ferry departure times are not coordinated. Buses depart for the town of Jindo from Haenam, Mokpo, Gwangju, Busan, and Seoul.

How to Get to Gwanmae-do from Paengmok-hang

 a) Multiple ferries are available from the Paengmok-hang on Jin-do. For the ferries departing at 9:30 am, the journey time is two and a half hours at a cost of 13,000 won. For those departing at noon and 3 pm, the trip is one hour and fifteen minutes at a cost of 9,500 won. According to the operator, boat services increase to five departures daily for a very short period during the summer (from late July to mid-August) to accommodate vacationers. Departure times and routes may change at the discretion of the operator. Ticket sales are based on first come first serve and are available only one hour before the departure.

b) From Mokpo Coastal Ferry Terminal, a ferry departs for Gwanmae-do once daily at 8:30 am. The journey takes up to seven hours, as the boat stops at other islands en route. The cost is 23,300 won (see How to Get to Mokpo Coastal Ferry Terminal on p. 105).

TIP

Korea at Its Best!

Hong-do, Heuksan-do, and Gageo-do 가거도 are the three most popular islands toured by Koreans, but Gwanmae-do 관매도 is this author's pick. This naturally preserved island with minimal human impact offers a beautiful, peaceful spot.

Yeompo Beach
Campground
염포 야영장

⌂ 312 Oecho-ri, Bongnae-myeon,
Goheung-gun, Jeollanam-do
℡ 061-835-7828
🕐 Open all year round

Cold enough in winter to form sheets of ice on ponds, but warm enough in summer for the growing palm trees, Yeompo Campground in Naro-do district is distant from major cities and expressways and offers campers the experience of a getaway into the lifestyle of quiet village communities. Located 7 km from the fishing village of Naro-do and facing westward along a black pebble beach, this campground has two grassy tiers upon which to pitch tents. There are two field kitchens, a shower trailer, and a bathroom block. The parking lot is 25 m from the campground, so campers must carry their gear onto their site. On the outskirts of Naro-do is a ranger station should visitors require information, and in town tour boats operate during peak season.

Transport Info   From Route 2 (about halfway between Suncheon 순천 and Boseong 보성 and just south of the town of Beolgyo 벌교), take Route 77 going south toward the small city of Goheung 고흥. At Goheung, exit onto Route 15 and follow the road signs to Naro-do 나로도 and Oenaro-do 외나로도. The campground is on Oenaro-do about 7 km past the village of Naro-do.

  Buses depart Naro-do Bus Terminal (six times daily) for Yeompo Beach Campground. The first bus leaves at 6:00 am, the last at 6:10 pm. Buses for the village of Naro-do depart from Goheung (ten times daily), Gwangju, Yeosu, Suncheon, and Busan. Goheung is a major transit point for this region, servicing Seoul, Busan and Gwangju. Getting to Yeompo Beach Campground requires a two- or three-bus transfer.

Halla-san
National Park
한라산 국립공원

Highlights

1. Hike to the top of **Seongsan Ilchulbong** 성산일출봉 **volcanic crater** for the scenic sea views. This is one of Korea's prime locations for people to gather to watch the sunrise, especially on New Year's Day.

2. Explore the vast underground **Manjang Cave** 만장굴, which stretch for a kilometer in length. Staircases and walkways with appropriate lighting have been built to make exploration safe.

3. Tour **U-do** 우도 on foot or by bus. Golf carts and bycicles are also for hire at the ferry dock. One can find on this island narrow lanes to explore, fine white sand beaches, peanut farms, a haenyeo village, and lots of wind. The harbor for U-do ferries is located just 2 km from Seongsan Ilchulbong.

4. Climb **Halla-san** 한라산. There are some lovely forest and alpine routes to discover.

5. Visit a museum—or two or three. While Jeju City operates a terrific **National Museum** 제주국립박물관, there are also other smaller museums dotting the island, including the **Haenyeo Museum** 해녀 박물관 in Hado-ri and the **O'Sulloc Tea Museum** 오설록 티 뮤지엄 west of Halla-san.

Jeju Island is one of the top tourist destinations in all of Korea. As of 2007, it
had three places listed as UNESCO World Heritage Sites: Halla-san National
Park, the Geomunoreum 거문오름 lava tube system (or Manjang Cave 만장굴), and
the Seongsan Ilchulbong 성산일출봉 volcanic crater. Furthermore, Jeju Island was
selected in 2011 as one of the New Seven Wonders of Nature. Chosen from
among 28 natural sites around the world, the other winning contenders included
the Amazon River in Brazil, Ha Long Bay in Vietnam, and Iguazu Falls in
Argentina.

Thousands of years ago, volcanic eruptions spurted lava across this now bell-
shaped island. For later human inhabitants, these eruptions left behind black,
jagged rock and fertile soil. From these raw materials, people planted crops, built
their homes, erected dry stone field walls, and carved the *dolhareubang* 돌하르방
(stone grandfather statues) that even today can be seen standing outside houses
to offer protection and fertility. It is the black lava stone that makes this island
uniquely different from the mainland and that leaves a lasting impression on
travelers.

Just 85 km south of the mainland, this semi-oceanic island has a fickle climate that requires visitors to be prepared for rapid weather changes in the course of a single day. Near and around Seogwipo 서귀포, it is warm enough for farmers to grow citrus, bananas, and pineapples. In the winter, seaside farmers produce hardier crops like cabbage, potatoes, and carrots. But at the summit of Halla-san, the highest peak in all of Korea at 1,950 m, snow is abundant in the winter. In just one day, travelers can trek through knee-deep snow in the morning and be walking among citrus orchards by the afternoon. When spring does finally arrive, the island is painted with yellow canola, pink azalea, and, in the mountains, small delicate alpine flowers.

Haenyeo, the women divers of Jeju Island (top)
Jeju traditional dwelling with *dolhareubang* (bottom)

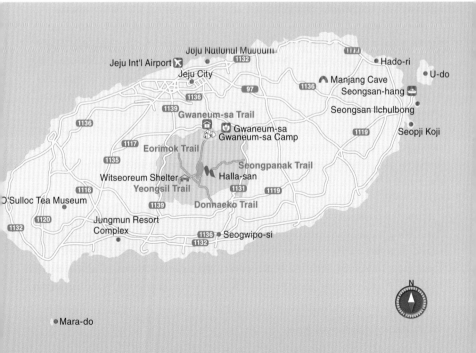

Jeju National Museum
Jeju Int'l Airport
Jeju City
Hado-ri
U-do
Manjang Cave
Seongsan-hang
Seongsan Ilchulbong
Gwaneum-sa Trail
Gwaneum-sa
Gwaneum-sa Camp
Seopji Koji
Eorimok Trail
Seongpanak Trail
Witseoreum Shelter
Halla-san
Yeongsil Trail
Donnaeko Trail
O'Sulloc Tea Museum
Jungmun Resort Complex
Seogwipo-si
Mara-do

1132 1177 1136 1119 97 1136 1139 1136 1117 1135 1116 1120 1132 1139 1131 1119 1136 1132

Hikers make their way up to Halla-san peak.

It is said that Jeju Island has an abundance of stones, wind, and women. Although no one would argue the first and second points, the third requires further explanation. Fishing is one of the island's main livelihoods, and when the men leave for sea, the women are left behind to tend to the fields and home. Historically unique to Jeju, with a history dating as far back as the 17th century, are the women divers called *haenyeo* 해녀. Although fewer younger women take to this profession today, opting instead for an easier life, you can still see (especially along the east coast) women divers whose only gear is their mask, flippers, pick, and hand basket. These women are known to hold their breath for up to two minutes while gathering various kinds of seafood from the rocky seabed. Similarly to a cooperative arrangement, the *haenyeo* share their catch among themselves. Jeju has a long history of female contributions to community and home life that still remains evident today.

From the *haenyeo* to Halla-san, the lava tube caves, and the Seongsan Ilchulbong crater, there are plenty of sights and activities to enjoy across the island. Jeju has a 250 kilometer-long bicycle path, scuba diving opportunities, some great museums, intimate beach coves, and a not-to-be-missed side excursion to U-do 우도, where they grow peanuts! Ride a Mongolian pony, walk through a

folk village, take a sightseeing boat tour, or place a bet at the horse racetrack—Jeju Island is a veritable playground with something for every age group.

Halla-san National Park is easy to reach, with its location at the very heart of the island. Jeju City is located several kilometers north of the park boundary. There are up to five trails in the national park leading to the summit of Halla-san. Some are more challenging than others, while others require more endurance. Trails are sometimes closed for natural restoration or due to an unexpected occurrence. The national park trails are Gwaneum-sa 관음사 (8.7 km), Eorimok 어리목 (6.8 km), Yeongsil 영실 (5.8 km), Donnaeko 돈내코 (7 km), and Seongpanak 성판악 (9.6 km). Jeju Bus Terminal has bus service to all trails, although not all bus routes stop in front of the trailhead. Hikers should expect short to long walks to reach their trailhead choice. Do note that the final ascent to the summit of Halla-san is closed every few years for natural restoration. Don't let this discourage you—the trail to Witseoreum Shelter 윗세오름 대피소 near the summit base has some spectacular views. Contact the park's department for maps and updates on trail closures and conditions.

 Gwaneum-sa (064-724-6830, http://Jjejugwaneumsa.or.kr)

Transport Info

How to Get to Jeju Island
 Multiple flights to Jeju City are available from various airports around the country. Jeju is served by Jeju Air, Jin Air, Air Busan, Eastar Jet, T'way, Asiana Airlines, and Korean Air (see Airline on p. 32).

Ferries depart for Jeju-do from Mokpo (five hours), Wando (three hours), Busan (up to fifteen hours), Yeosu (three and a half hours), and Incheon (sixteen and a half hours). Some transport cars, while others make express runs. Ferry schedules vary depending on the season and weather conditions. Most ships offer three classes, from ondol (under-floor heating) and airline-style seats to comfortable cabins (see Ferry on p. 33).

Traveling Around Jeju
 For those wishing to see the various sights around the island, Jeju has well-established bus routes going to all regions. Buses No. 100 and 300 run between the airport and bus terminal.

 Another popular option is to rent a car, though reservations are required, especially during peak season (see Car Rental on p. 30).

Gwaneum-sa
Campground
관음사 야영장

⌂ Odeung-dong, Jeju-si, Jeju-do
✆ 064-756-9950
🕐 April to November

Entrance Fee: Free

Camping Fee (Unit: KRW)

Type	Fee
Small (1–3 people)	3,000
Medium (4–9 people)	4,500
Large (10+ people)	6,000

(per tent per night)

Parking Fee (Unit: KRW)

Type of Vehicle	Rate
Two wheels	500
Small vehicles (displacement below 1,000 cc)	1,000
Cars (loading capacity under 4t)	1,800
Small bus (11–15 seats)	3,000
Mid-large bus (freight over 4t) (more than 16 seats)	3,700

(per vehicle per night)

Gwaneum-sa Campground is located in a forested district halfway between Regional Roads 1139 and 1131 along Regional Road 1117 on the north side of Halla-san National Park.

With two bathroom blocks, a kitchen, and a shower block, this campground can accommodate up to 70 tents depending on size and spacing. This place is very popular during the summer, so it is strongly recommended that you make reservations. A ranger station is located on site should travelers have any questions about the trails. The Gwaneum-sa Trail starts from behind the park office. There is a small convenience store across the road, but visitors are advised to pack their own food.

Wild deer

Transport Info From Jeju Airport, make a left turn out of the parking lot. Drive to the first intersection and turn right. Follow the signs to Regional Road 1139 and Jungmun Resort 중문관광단지. Drive for a few kilometers south of Jeju City along 1139 before making a left turn onto Regional Road 1117.

 a) Buses depart from Jeju Bus Terminal between 6 am and 9:30 pm on post No. 6 (make sure to confirm the bus destination prior to boarding). The bus stop is 3.3 km from the campground. Tell the driver to let you off at the nearest stop to Gwaneum-sa. Campers must walk the remaining distance. The campground is located a kilometer past Gwaneum-sa.

b) Bus No. 1 runs directly to the campground every Sunday and every second and fourth Saturday of the month. The bus stop is located directly in front of the campground. The park attendant said that campers can catch this bus near Jeju City Hall.

 Taxis charge a flat rate of about 15,000 won to go from Jeju Airport to the campground.

Halla-san is surrounded by *oreum*, or parasitic volcanic cones.

Essential Korean for Campers

Polite Basics

Hello.	Annyeong hasimnikka? (formal)	안녕하십니까?
	Annyeong haseyo. (informal)	안녕하세요.
Goodbye.	Annyeong-hi gaseyo. (to person leaving)	안녕히 가세요.
	Annyeong-hi gyeseyo. (to person staying)	안녕히 계세요.
Yes.	Ne/Ye.	네/예.
No.	Aniyo.	아니요.
Please...	...Haejuseyo. (say it at the end of a request)	...해주세요.
Thank you.	Gamsa hamnida.	감사합니다.
You're welcome.	Cheonmaneyo.	천만에요.
Excuse me.	Sillye hamnida.	실례합니다.
Sorry.	Joesong hamnida.	죄송합니다.

Questions

Excuse me.	Sillye hamnida.	실례합니다.
I'm looking for a...	...reul/eul chatgo isseoyo.	...를/을 찾고 있어요.

- guesthouse minbakjib 민박집
- tourist office gwangwang annaeso 관광안내소
- ranger station gong-won samuso 공원사무소

Where is...?	...eodie isseoyo?	...어디에 있어요?

- national park gungnip gongwon 국립공원
- campground yayeongjang 야영장
- bathroom hwajangsil 화장실
- supermarket syupermaket 슈퍼마켓

How much is it?	...eolmayeyo?	…얼마예요?

- per night   harut bam   하룻밤
- per person   han saram   한 사람

Can I camp here?	Yeogiseo yayeonghaedo doemnikka? 여기서 야영해도 됩니까?
Do you speak English?	Yeong-eo haseyo? 영어 하세요?
Is this the road to...?	Igil ttaragamyeon ...e galsu isseoyo? 이 길 따라가면 …에 갈 수 있어요?
Please write it down.	jeogeo juseyo. 적어 주세요.
Please fill it up.	gadeuk chaewo juseyo. 가득 채워 주세요.

- diesel   dijel   디젤
- gas/petrol   hwibalyu   휘발유

I'd like (10) litres.	(sip) liter neo-eo juseyo. (십) 리터 넣어 주세요.
I need a mechanic.	jeongbigong-i piryo haeyo. 정비공이 필요해요.

Dates and Time

Monday	woryoil	월요일	Tuesday	hwayoil	화요일
Wednesday	suyoil	수요일	Thursday	mogyoil	목요일
Friday	geumyoil	금요일	Saturday	toyoil	토요일
Sunday	iryoil	일요일			

today	oneul	오늘	yesterday	eojae	어제
tomorrow	nae-il	내일	When?	eonjae	언제

Numbers

	Sino-Korean		Native Korean	
0	영/공	yeong/gong	–	–
1	일	il	하나	hana
2	이	i	둘	dul
3	삼	sam	셋	set
4	사	sa	넷	net
5	오	o	다섯	daseot
6	육	yuk	여섯	yeoseot
7	칠	chil	일곱	ilgop
8	팔	pal	여덟	yeodeol
9	구	gu	아홉	ahop
10	십	sip	열	yeol
11	십일	sibil	열 하나	yeol hana
12	십이	sibi	열 둘	yeol dul
13	십삼	sipsam	열 셋	yeol set
14	십사	sipsa	열 넷	yeol net
15	십오	sibo	열 다섯	yeol daseot
16	십육	simnyuk	열 여섯	yeol yeoseot
17	십칠	sipchil	열 일곱	yeol ilgop
18	십팔	sippal	열 여덟	yeol yeodeol
19	십구	sipgu	열 아홉	yeol ahop
20	이십	isip	스물	seumul
30	삼십	samsip	서른	seoreun
40	사십	sasip	마흔	maheun
50	오십	osip	쉰	swin
60	육십	yuksip	예순	yesun
70	칠십	chilsip	일흔	ilheun
80	팔십	palsip	여든	yeodeun
90	구십	gusip	아흔	aheun
100	백	baek	온	on
1,000	천	cheon	즈믄	jeumeun
10,000	만	man	드먼	deumeon
100,000,000	억	eok	잘	jal

Directions

North	bukjjok	북쪽	South	namjjok	남쪽
East	dongjjok	동쪽	West	seojjok	서쪽
Left	oenjjok	왼쪽	Right	oreunjjok	오른쪽

Go straight.	Jikjin haseyo.	직진하세요.
Turn left.	Oeonjjok-euro gaseyo.	왼쪽으로 가세요.
Turn right.	Oreunjjok-euro gaseyo.	오른쪽으로 가세요.
Go up.	Wijjok-euro gaseyo.	위쪽으로 가세요.
Go down.	Araejjok-euro gaseyo.	아래쪽으로 가세요.
I'm lost.	Gireul ireosseoyo.	길을 잃었어요.

Transportation

Please take me to…	…gajuseyo	…가주세요.
How can I get to…?	…e eotteoke gayo?	…에 어떻게 가요?
What time does the… leave/arrive?	…eonjae tteonayo/dochak-haeyo?	…언제 떠나요 / 도착해요?

• bus	beoseu	버스
• bus station	beoseu jeongryujang	버스 정류장
• train	gicha	기차
• train station	gichayeok	기차역
• airplane	bihaeng-gi	비행기
• airport	gonghang	공항
• airport bus	gonghang beoseu	공항버스
• ferry boat	yeogaekseon	여객선
• ticket	pyo	표

A ticket to…, please.	…euro ganeun pyo juseyo.	…으로 가는 표 주세요.

Food

Not too spicy, please.

Neomu maepji anke ha juseyo.
너무 맵지 않게 해주세요.

It was delicious.

Masisseosseo-yo.
맛있었어요.

• gimbap	김밥	rice wrap with vegetables cut into slices
• kimchi	김치	fermented cabbage
• bulgogi	불고기	barbequed beef or pork slices
• dakgalbi	닭갈비	spicy chicken grilled with vegetables and rice cakes
• bibimguksu	비빔국수	noodles with vegetables, meat and sauce
• japchae	잡채	stir fried noodles with vegetables
• bap	밥	boiled rice
• bibimbap	비빔밥	rice topped with egg, meat, vegetables and sauce
• boribap	보리밥	boiled rice with steamed barley and vegetables
• sanchae bibimbap	산채비빔밥	*bibimbap* with mountain vegetables
• ssambap	쌈밥	assorted ingredients with rice and leaf wraps
• chobap	초밥	sushi
• nakji	낙지	octopus
• ojing-eo	오징어	squid
• mae-un-tang	매운탕	spicy fish soup
• bosintang	보신당	dog meat soup
• bindaetteok	빈대떡	mung bean pancake
• pajeon	파전	green onion pancake
• cha	차 / 녹차	tea/green tea
• mul	물	water
• juseu	주스	juice
• keopi	커피	coffee
• soju	소주	distilled rice wine, like vodka
• maekju	맥주	beer
• bokbunja	복분자	mountain berry wine
• makgeolli	막걸리	creamy rice wine

Emergencies

| Help! | Dowa juseyo! | 도와주세요! |
| Call... | ...bulleo juseyo! | ···불러주세요! |

- a doctor — uisa — 의사
- the police — gyeongchal — 경찰
- an ambulance — gugeupcha — 구급차

| I'm sick. | Apayo. | 아파요. |

- headache — dutong — 두통
- diarrhea — seolsa — 설사
- stomachache — boktong — 복통
- food poisoning — sikjungdok — 식중독
- fever — yeol — 열

Important Places

- a temple — jeol — 절
- a swimming pool — suyeongjang — 수영장
- a bathhouse — onuna or jjimjilbang — 사우나 / 찜질방
- a convenience store — pyeonuijeom — 편의점
- a pharmacy — yakguk — 약국
- a post office — ucheguk — 우체국
- a hospital — byeong-won — 병원
- a mountain — san — 산
- a valley — gyegok — 계곡
- a gorge — gol — 골
- a river — gang — 강
- a pass — jae — 재
- a water spring — saem — 샘
- a hiking trail — deungsanno — 등산로
- a hiking store — deungsan yongpum gage — 등산용품 가게
- an Internet café — PC bang — PC 방
- a bank — eunhaeng — 은행
- a restaurant — sikdang — 식당

Acknowledgements

I want to extend my gratitude to Jody Shipton, who brought to the discussion table a realistic perspective on what this writing project would entail. I also want to thank her for her positive feedback and support throughout the project.

Two versions of this book were written, the first freely composed while camping. The second version was written after Michelle Alkana made invaluable recommendations. She brought clarity and order to this book and made important corrections. Michelle's ideas and suggestions were very much appreciated and diligently applied.

I want to thank Yoon Myeong-keum for meticulously editing the Korean language used in the glossary, titles, and transliteration of names. I am genuinely grateful for the time Myeong-keum took out of her busy schedule to provide corrections and feedback.

To my niece Megan Andrew, who is a talented photographer, I want to express my appreciation for allowing me to use several of her photographs in this book.

Thank you to Alma on Docho-do, and to Jimmy in Danyang. Out of the goodness of their hearts, these two people walked with me and helped me gather valuable transportation information on Dadohae-haesang and Worak-san National Parks.

I want to extend my sincere gratitude to the Korea National Park Service for providing scenic photos for the book. Also, many thanks to all the KNPS staff members like Christina, Shin Myung-sik, and Kim Myung-jin who provided key information on parks. Without the help of KNPS staff, this book would not have become a reality.

Finally, a very special thanks to the Seoul Selection team for taking this project under their wing.

Credits

Writer & Photographer	Beverlee Barnet

Publisher	Kim Hyung-geun
Editor	Kim Eugene
Copy-editor	Colin Mouat
Proofreader	Robert Koehler

Designer	Jung Hyun-young
Cartographers	Jung Hyun-young, Park Min-cheol

Additional Photo Credits

Korea National Park Service	14, 29, 39, 43, 44, 46, 51, 53, 59, 60, 68, 72, 74, 80, 86, 87, 88, 92, 109, 116, 117, 120, 128, 130, 137, 138, 142, 144, 146, 149, 154, 158, 160, 167
Bukhansan National Park	39
Byeonsanbando National Park	162, 164, 165
Chiaksan National Park	99, 100, 102, 103, 104, 105
Dadohaehaesang National Park	179, 180, 182, 187, 188
Deogyusan National Park	155, 158, 159
Gayasan National Park	121, 124, 125
Gyerongsan National Park	67
Hallyehaesang National Park	145, 149, 151
Jirisan National Park	22, 129, 132, 134, 135, 136, 141
Naejangsan National Park	166, 167, 168, 169, 170, 171
Odaesan National Park	93, 94, 96, 97
Seoraksan National Park	64, 91
Sobaeksan National Park	45, 48
Songnisan National Park	61, 62, 65
Taeanhaean National Park	18, 25, 73, 76, 79, 82
Wolchulsan National Park	173, 174, 175
Woraksan National Park	26, 56, 57
Korea Tourism Organization	41, 45, 87, 93, 99, 119, 161, 167, 179
Jeju Special Self-Governing Province	190, 191, 192, 193, 194, 197
Yeongam County	173
Yonhap Photo	38, 51, 73, 99, 109, 115, 121,150, 155, 161, 167
Image Today	14, 45, 51, 54, 61, 67, 87, 93, 98, 108, 110, 115, 129, 145, 179
Robert Koehler	26, 40, 45, 113, 114, 115, 118, 155, 156, 161
Ryu Seung-hoo	14, 73, 90, 121, 122, 125, 148
Kang Min-kyu	42
Kim Ilmo	196